Unpuzzling Your Life

UNPUZZLING YOUR *Life*

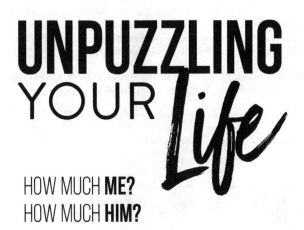

HOW MUCH **ME?**
HOW MUCH **HIM?**

SANDRA P. HASTINGS

NASHVILLE

NEW YORK • LONDON • MELBOURNE • VANCOUVER

UNPUZZLING YOUR *Life*

How Much Me? How Much Him?

Published in New York, New York, by Morgan James Publishing. Morgan James is a trademark of Morgan James, LLC. www.MorganJamesPublishing.com

All Scripture is taken from the King James Version of the Holy Bible.

Proudly distributed by Ingram Publisher Services.

Morgan James BOGO™

A **FREE** ebook edition is available for you or a friend with the purchase of this print book.

CLEARLY SIGN YOUR NAME ABOVE

Instructions to claim your free ebook edition:
1. Visit MorganJamesBOGO.com
2. Sign your name CLEARLY in the space above
3. Complete the form and submit a photo of this entire page
4. You or your friend can download the ebook to your preferred device

ISBN 9781631956171 paperback
ISBN 9781631956188 ebook
Library of Congress Control Number: 2021907785

Cover and Interior Design by:
Chris Treccani
www.3dogcreative.net

Morgan James is a proud partner of Habitat for Humanity Peninsula and Greater Williamsburg. Partners in building since 2006.

Get involved today! Visit MorganJamesPublishing.com/giving-back

Table of Contents

Introduction

Lord, what is wrong? Are You angry with me? The harder I try to please You, the less peace I feel. I don't understand what is happening and feel confused and frustrated. These were some of my thoughts as a young missionary wife and mother when the Lord began turning my life upside-down.

Two months after Thomas and I were married, God placed His call in our hearts to go to the mission field. Following graduation from a university in Pueblo, Colorado, we prepared to pursue that call. We spent three years in Bible college. For two of those years, my husband pastored a small country church, and I worked as a registered nurse at one of the nearby hospitals. In the middle of all this our Lord gave us two beautiful children.

Following graduation, my husband traveled thousands of miles visiting many churches and presenting the need for the gospel in Germany. The Lord blessed, and in fifteen months we had our needed financial support.

At last, after spending five years preparing, we were ready to go to Germany as missionaries. We were excited and convinced this was God's will for our lives. After saying good-bye to our family, friends, and home church, we left America and everything we knew behind us. On December 6, 1971, we arrived in Germany full of zeal to do God's will. It did not take long, however, to realize zeal alone was not enough.

Learning the German language and adjusting to a foreign culture were challenging, to say the least. Then the Lord brought an unexpected blessing into our lives: a third baby. During this time, an American military church asked my husband to be their interim pastor and help them get a pastor from the States. My husband accepted this position, and it took ten months for a new pastor to arrive at the church.

Finally, we could focus our attention on what we came to Germany to do. We moved to a new town and began the difficult and challenging work of starting a church from ground zero. My husband spent hours in the city visiting, meeting people, and passing out literature. Slowly, one by one a small group of people began meeting in a rented building, and a new church was taking shape.

The next three years were packed with endless activity, frequent guests, and learning to teach Sunday school and ladies' meetings in German. On top of it all came the care of three young children. The stress and pressure I felt increased as did my weariness. Then a significant, unexpected, unwanted change took place.

I developed health issues that hindered me from accomplishing the work for which I felt responsible. As a result, my self-esteem decreased. This led to discouragement, guilt, and an ever-increasing sense of failure. I had no joy and could only see what I was not getting done. This situation accelerated. After getting counsel from our pastor in the States, we decided to leave the mission field and return to America.

After a year filled with doctor's visits, medical tests, and a hospital stay, it was clear I could not go back to Germany. The doctor called it a physical breakdown caused by burning the candle at both ends. But that was not the whole story.

My husband resigned as a missionary, and it appeared this chapter of our life was over. This decision broke our hearts. I felt overwhelmed with confusion and guilt. Why was this happening? What did I do wrong? What was the Lord doing?

From a young age I wanted to serve the Lord and tried with all my heart to do so. Now it felt as if it were to no avail. Flooded with questions, I slowly shifted my focus to myself, as the dark, cold walls of depression closed in.

Sometimes, despite reading God's Word and going to church, life gets perplexing. We know Scripture and yet have difficulty connecting it to our daily lives. We struggle to decipher the difference between God's will and our own, while human reasoning challenges our faith.

Have you ever had your world turned upside-down? Has God brought circumstances and heartaches into your life that did not make sense to you? Have you found yourself depressed and questioning God's plan and the purpose of your own life while wondering what God expects from you?

If you have had questions such as these, then this Bible study is for you. By comparing life to a puzzle, this study will help you find the answers to these questions and you will learn more about the One who designed your unique life. You will discover how carefully your Designer orchestrates situations and circumstances and that your self-worth does not lie in what you do but in who you are. This study will inspire you to deepen your love relationship with your Designer, Jesus Christ, and to be thankful for being a unique child of God.

Chapter One
POWER OF DESIGN

Imagine giving someone an undetermined amount of time to put a puzzle together without telling them the total number of pieces or the size of the puzzle or showing them a picture of how it should look when finished. Now give them only one random piece at a time. What are their chances of completing the designed picture? We might protest that this is an impossibility; yet it is precisely the dilemma we face in life.

Unexpected events, sudden changes, unexplainable encounters, victories and defeats, sickness and death take place in every believer's life. Like pieces in a puzzle, each one has a designed place and purpose, but how do they fit together? Who determines the piece to add and when?

Human limitations make it impossible for us to know the answer to these questions. Only the Designer of our life puzzle,

Jesus Christ, has the answers we seek. If He is the Designer of our puzzle, then He started with a divine design.

Design critics often say design is one of the most powerful forces in our lives. This statement doesn't make sense unless we understand what design is and what makes it so powerful.

Design is a method worked out in advance before a project begins, and nothing of use, beauty, or benefit develops without it. It is what makes the difference between mediocre and exceptional. Now let's take a look at the divine design that makes us and our world so incredible.

DAY 1
SUPER BRAIN

Humanity is exquisitely unique. When our Designer created nature, animal life, and the universe, He just spoke, and they came into existence. The creation of man, however, was different.

With His mighty hands the Designer scooped up some earth and, with perfect precision, formed man—a human being made in His likeness. "And God said, Let us make man in our image, after our likeness" (Genesis 1:26).

Then He breathed into man the breath of life. "And the Lord God formed man of the dust of the ground, and breathed into his nostrils the breath of life; and man became a living soul" (Genesis 2:7).

A worthless bit of dust in the Master Designer's hands became a remarkable work of excellence. Let's take a closer look at the intricate design and engineering of our human body. It excels far above any construction of man. The best scientists and engineers have not come close to replicating its beauty, performance, or complexity.

Our brain is one example of marvelous excellence. It works in tandem with our nervous system enabling us to feel the spectrum of human emotion from tremendous grief and despair to happiness and ecstasy. The brain, the chemicals it releases, and its relationship to the nervous system are responsible for every emotion we experience. Messages from the brain travel along the nerves at speeds up to two hundred miles an hour.

Our brains contain eighty-six billion nerve cells, and they are all joined together by more connections than the number of stars in the Milky Way. Just think about the intricate design involved.

Some have tried to compare the human brain to a computer. If the brain were a computer, it could perform thirty-eight thousand trillion operations per second. The newest supercomputer, OLCF-4, introduced in June 2019, is said to come close to doing this many operations in a second. But significant differences remain.

The supercomputer requires two tennis courts in floor space and five million watts of energy, not to mention a massive cooling system. It is not portable and requires a large staff of technicians to keep it on track.

The human brain is the size of two fists, requires fifteen watts of energy, weighs 1.5 kilograms, and is always with us. It needs no human technician to maintain it and can even re-program itself. Obviously, the design behind our brain is far superior to anything man can create.

Our brain enables us to learn at all levels. It keeps our natural body functions working, coordinates our body based on sensory input (unconsciously), gives us self-awareness, and enables us to think. Many of these processes are often going on all at the same time.

Coupled with the ability to think comes the ability to create and make choices. We can gather information, analyze, compare, and process to draw a conclusion. Everything that takes place in our conscious mind connects to our will and subconscious.

Our Designer did not create robots. He designed and created a being in His likeness with immense capabilities and a free will. He gave us the ability and the freedom to make choices in all areas of our life, including our relationship to Him.

Ryan Whitwam, a known skeptic and former research scientist, said, "The human mind could not create an object that could exhibit the powers of the human brain. It has a designer capable of feats unfathomable to humans."[1]

If we think back to what we said about the power of design, it is evident that our Designer had an excellent design for our brain and its unsurpassed abilities.

"But now, O Lord, thou art our father; we are the clay, and thou our potter; and we all are the work of thy hand" (Isaiah 64:8).

Dig Deeper:

- Why do you think our Designer gives us free will? Write out your answer.
- What does David say about our Designer's interest in us? (Psalm 139:13-17)
- Why do you think our Designer gives us intelligence and understanding? (Psalm 119:73)
- What do you think your Designer wants you to do with your mental abilities?

My Thoughts:

_____

_____

_____

_____

_____

_____

_____

_____

_____

_____

_____

_____

_____

_____

_____

_____

_____

_____

_____

_____

_____

_____

_____

_____

_____

_____

_____

_____

_____

_____
_____
_____
_____
_____
_____
_____
_____
_____
_____
_____
_____
_____
_____
_____
_____
_____
_____
_____
_____
_____
_____
_____
_____
_____
_____
_____
_____
_____
_____

DAY 2
THE INCREDIBLE RED LIFELINE

Our brain is not the only remarkable part of our body. Our blood is one of the most amazing substances in the world, and every one of the thirty trillion cells in our body depends on it. It takes approximately sixty thousand miles of blood vessels to carry this fantastic life-giving liquid to and from these cells. If all the vessels were placed end to end, they could wrap around the earth nearly two-and-a-half times. One drop of blood can travel from your heart through your body and back to your heart in only sixty seconds.

Blood has three main components—red blood cells or erythrocytes, white blood cells called leukocytes, and platelets. The red cells carry needed oxygen and nutrients from our lungs to the cells, and on the return trip they take carbon dioxide and waste products from the cells. On an interesting side note, the waste gas we exhale through our lungs is what plants around us need to survive. And the gas these plants produce is oxygen...exactly what we need to live. Accident or incredible design?

Nearly two million red blood cells die every second, and at the same time this amount is produced by our bone marrow and released into our blood stream. How long they live is determined by various chemicals in our body and our environment.

Our white cells, called leukocytes, are like little soldiers. Our Designer has given them built-in orders to circulate through our body on the lookout for viruses, bacteria, and other foreign invaders threatening our health. One particular type of leukocyte rolls along the walls of the blood vessels. If they find harmful bacteria, they destroy it by engulfing them. When our body is in distress, and a particular area is under attack, white cells rush together to fight against the danger.

The platelets are the smallest in size, and they cause our blood to clot. They know where and when to group together, forming a plug when there is a hole in a vessel like when we cut our finger peeling potatoes. These three elements never get confused about their functions or need us to direct them. They are already precisely programmed.

Our blood is not only amazing, but we cannot live without it. "For the life of the flesh is in the blood" (Leviticus 17:11). Science has managed to make artificial hearts, kidneys, knees, ears, eyes, and various other organs, but there is no replacement for human blood.

Just as our physical body cannot live without blood, we cannot live spiritually without the blood of Christ. It is His shed blood on the cross that gives us new, eternal, spiritual life. "Forasmuch as ye know that ye were not redeemed with corruptible things, as silver and gold, from your vain conversation received by tradition from your fathers, but with the precious blood of Christ, as of a lamb without blemish and without spot" (1 Peter 1:18-19).

Only our divine Master Designer could create this incredible red lifeline with its minute details and unsurpassed efficiency.

Dig Deeper:
- Why do you think God told the Israelites to put blood on the doorposts in Exodus 12:13? What do you think it represented?
- What do these amazing facts about our blood tell you about our Designer?
- How does knowing Christ shed His blood to give you spiritual, eternal life make you feel? Write out your thoughts and feelings.
- What value do you think we should put on life and, in particular, on our own lives?

My Thoughts:

_____

_____

_____

_____

_____

_____

_____

_____

_____

_____

_____

_____

_____

_____

_____

_____

_____

_____

_____

_____

_____

_____

_____

_____

_____

_____

_____

_____
_____
_____
_____
_____
_____
_____
_____
_____
_____
_____
_____
_____
_____
_____
_____
_____
_____
_____
_____
_____
_____
_____
_____
_____
_____
_____
_____
_____

DAY 3
DETAILED UNIQUENESS

According to the multi-disciplinary designer, Alvalyn Lundgren, if the design is to hit the target, it needs to be custom made and one-of-a-kind.[2] Taking this thought into account, let's see if our Designer hit the target when He designed you and me.

Just by simple observation, we see that no two people are exactly alike. Approximately 7.8 billion people are alive today. If we consider all the people who have lived since Adam, keeping in mind that each one was uniquely different, we can see our Designer has a boundless imagination and creative ability.

How far does our uniqueness go? We all have facial features and a body; yet the size, shape, color, and arrangement of these features make us look different. We have diverse personalities, abilities, talents, intelligence, and interests. We were born and grew up in a wide variety of places, cultures, climates, and social standings.

Our differences get specific. Each of us has a distinct fingerprint, and the print of each of our fingers differs from the other. Our DNA is exclusive, and the voices we are born with are different. Even identical twins have minute differences that make them one-of-a-kind.

It is vitally important for us to accept our individuality and realize we are designed uniquely on purpose and not intended to be alike. Society tends to label people who differ from the so-called norm as mistakes, undesirable or even without value. Is this true? Does the Designer not have control over life? Are some differences accidents? Let's consider some famous people of our day who do not fit in the norm category.

Nicholas Vujicic was born without arms or legs. At his birth, his parents and church family couldn't understand why God would allow him to be born with this condition. In time, however, they accepted him as God's gift and believed God had a plan for his life.

Nick struggled with his condition and wrestled with why he was different from all the other kids. At the age of ten, he tried to drown himself in the bathtub but did not succeed. Without a doubt, his young years were hard.

In his Designer's timing and orchestrating of circumstances and events, Nick came to know Christ as his Savior at the age of fourteen. He still did not know the why of his condition but was convinced his Designer simply wanted his trust. As the pieces of his puzzle began coming together, Nick could see the purpose. "I have experienced that God's plans for us are much greater than our own ideas."[3]

Today Nick is married and has four beautiful children. He is a world-renowned motivational speaker and has shared his faith with more than four hundred million people. His books are now in more than thirty different languages. His unique difference was not an accident or a quirk of nature. Nick was made according to a divine design that he might have a powerful testimony.

I heard Frank Peretti, a well-known novel writer, speak at a Christian writers' conference. I was surprised and deeply moved as he shared his testimony about the difficulties of his childhood.

Frank suffered from cystic hygroma, and it spread to his tongue, causing it to turn black and become enlarged so that it protruded from his mouth. As a result, he endured much physical and verbal bullying during his early school years. The disease slowly improved. By his high school years, he could talk with his tongue staying in his mouth and began to develop his storytelling ability.

His Designer had a plan and continued to move needed pieces into Frank's puzzle and, in time, led him to write *This Present Darkness*. Writing did not come easy. Frank struggled with depression, poverty, and discouragement. Still, his Designer continued leading him to write. It took five years for Frank to complete the book, and it became an international bestseller. This book started his writing career.

The school shooting at Columbine High School in 1999 inspired Frank to write his only non-fiction book, titled *Wounded Spirit*. In this book he discusses the causes of youth violence and possible solutions. He also shares his traumatic childhood. This book was not only helpful for Frank but moved countless others toward personal healing. As the pieces of his puzzle began coming together, Frank recognized design.

Frank Peretti stated in an interview: "The Lord God knows what you're good at. He knows what you can do and what you can become. Trust Him."[4] Our Designer knows because He designed us. I have heard it said that God didn't make normal, just unique.

For one reason or another, many of us do not fit in the world's category of the norm, but one thing is sure. It is no accident that each of us is uniquely different. Regardless of our design, our purpose is the same. "Even every one that is called by my name: for I have created him for my glory, I have formed him; yea, I have made him" (Isaiah 43:7).

Our purpose is to bring glory to our Designer. "For by him were all things created, that are in heaven, and that are in earth, visible and invisible, whether they be thrones, or dominions, or principalities, or powers: all things were created by him, and for him" (Ephesians 1:16).

The unique design of our life puzzle will determine how we accomplish this. Each of us is in every way a marvelous one-of-a-kind.

Dig Deeper:

- Do you think John 9:3 could apply to Vujicic and Peretti? Explain your answer.
- Do you struggle with a handicap or limitation? Can you see how it could be used for God's glory?
- Fill in the blanks. Ephesians 2:10 says, "For we are _____ _____, created in Christ Jesus unto good works." What does this verse mean to you?
- How do you view people who are different from you?

My Thoughts:

_____

_____

_____

_____

_____

_____

_____

_____

_____

_____

_____

_____

_____

_____

_____

_____

_____

_____

_____

DAY 4
BALANCED UNIVERSE

Have you thought about our universe, about all the stars and planets, and wondered why they are as they are? I grew up in Colorado, and our family often spent weekends camping in the majestic Rocky Mountains. I loved to go out at night and gaze up at the sky. It looked like hundreds of diamonds sparkling against black velvet. It was breathtaking. "The heavens declare the glory of God; and the firmament sheweth his handywork" (Psalm 19:1).

Our universe is even more marvelous than it looks. By the end of 2001, astronomers had identified more than 150 finely tuned characteristics that would be necessary for intelligent physical life on earth.[5]

Our sun is a huge solitary star that gives off more energy every second than a billion major cities would use in an entire year. Yet it has just the right mass to allow it to burn hydrogen at a rate which will provide the earth with the amount and frequencies of light energy needed to maintain a biologically friendly temperature. Coincidence or design?

The earth rotates around the sun at nearly sixty-seven thousand miles per hour; yet it remains the perfect distance from it. At the same time, the earth is rotating on its axis, allowing the earth's entire surface to be warmed and cooled every day.

What about the moon? It is 240,000 miles from the earth, and it takes it one month to orbit the earth. It is the perfect size and distance from the earth for its gravitational pull to create ocean tides. These movements keep the oceans from stagnation and help restrain our massive oceans from flooding the continents around them.

Astronomers tell us the Milky Way has more than a hundred billion stars; yet this is only one galaxy. Innumerable galaxies contain a wide range of shapes and sizes. It is impossible for us to know the number of stars in the heavens, but someone does. The One who designed them also knows their names. "He telleth the number of the stars; he calleth them all by their names" (Psalm 147:4).

The distance between the stars is just right. If the gap were much smaller, the gravity of nearby stars could affect our solar system's stability, and nearby supernovas would bathe the earth with harmful doses of radiation.

Gravity remains constant, the earth rotates every twenty-four hours, the minutes tick away every day at a steady rate, the seasons change, but the speed of light does not vary. Hot coffee left on the cabinet will get cold, and milk chocolate left in the summer sun will melt. The laws of nature do not change. Balanced, detailed design in our universe is unmistakable.

Dig Deeper:
- What is the purpose of the sun and moon? (Genesis 1:14-18)
- Why did our Designer create the earth? (Isaiah 45:12, 18)
- For what purpose was the universe created? Read Psalm 19:1 and Psalm 97:6.
- How does Psalm 97:6 connect with Romans 1:20?
- What can you learn from identifying divine design in the world around you?

My Thoughts:

_____

_____

_____

_____

_____

_____

_____

_____

_____

_____

_____

_____

_____

_____

_____

_____

_____

_____

_____

_____

_____

_____

_____

_____

_____

_____

_____

DAY 5
METICULOUSLY DESIGNED NATURE

Imagine yourself in the middle of the Rocky Mountains, miles away from the noise of traffic jams, sirens, and screeching tires. You don't smell exhaust, roadside debris, or overturned garbage cans. Take a deep breath and give your lungs a long drink of fresh, clean air. Now listen closely, and you will hear the buzzing of busy little bees, birds cheerfully singing, and the whisper of the wind in the tall, majestic pines.

Whenever I had the opportunity to spend time in the mountains, I was overwhelmed with their beauty and grandeur. Fabulous is the only word I can think of to describe the design we can see and hear in nature. It is the ideal place to think about the words of Job. "Stand still, and consider the wondrous works of God" (Job 37:14).

Nature is not only beautiful, but many of God's creations baffle scientists. One of these extraordinary creations is birds. There are 9,956 known species of birds globally, and many of them can migrate thousands of miles with such accuracy that they land on the same nesting sites each year. Scientists do not know how they accomplish this feat. They seem to have an internal GPS. Many theories abound as to what makes this possible, but with no concrete explanation.

The fact is, birds have astonishing and unique navigational abilities. Even more incredible is that their Designer knows every time one of them falls. "Are not two sparrows sold for a farthing? And one of them shall not fall on the ground without your Father" (Matthew 10:29).

Bees use the sun as a compass to make navigational calculations. At night or on very cloudy days they rely on extensive patterns of polarized sky light. When clouds block or abbreviate these patterns, bees utilize a third option, their sixth sense, to guide them home. Research has found many animals possess this sixth sense. It is a magnetic field sensitivity, which is a backup navigation system. Bees have intricate, elaborate ways to navigate.

What about bats? Did you know a plugged ear can cause them to fly in confusing patterns? The explanation is that bats fly using sonar.

They emit as many as sixty supersonic sound pulses each second, which strike objects and bounce back to their ears. To calculate the locations of objects and direct their flying, bats use an accurate measure of the time required for the echo to return.

More amazingly, when bats send out their signals, their ear muscles automatically shut off their hearing so their radar can pick up only the guiding echoes. I am quite sure bats do not consciously think about all these processes. Their brains automatically know how to make the calculations needed.

No doubt, birds, bees, and bats did not engineer their abilities themselves. Each has an intricate, unique design made to fit their particular surroundings and needs. The same meticulous, creative Designer of nature designed you and me (Genesis 1:21-25; John 1:3).

Dig Deeper:
- If God created these small creatures with such careful, detailed design, how much interest do you think He takes in your design?
- Read Matthew 6:26; 10:29-31. What do these verses tell you about God's knowledge of you?
- What other examples in nature show a distinctive design?
- What conclusions about the Designer can you draw from nature?

My Thoughts:

_____

_____

_____

_____

_____

_____

_____

_____

_____

_____

_____

_____

_____

_____

_____

_____

_____

_____

_____

_____

_____

_____

_____

_____

_____

_____

_____

Chapter Two
REASONS FOR TRUST

I f we accept the fact that our Designer, Jesus Christ, designed our bodies and the world around us, then it stands to reason He also has a design—a plan and purpose—for our lives. True happiness, success, and fulfillment can only come when we accept the pieces our Designer places into our life puzzle and follow His leading.

The pieces He brings, however, do not always make sense to us. He may lead us through valleys of pain and suffering. The way may be steep and lonely. Accepting and following are not easy. How can we do it? It requires a heart of trust.

I accepted Christ as my personal Savior at the age of ten. In the years following, I learned a lot about Him and His Word. But we had a strained relationship because my perception of Him was built on fear and not on love. I knew things about Him from reading the Bible, but I didn't know Him.

When we sang the song "I Surrender All" in church, my eyes would fill with tears, and my insides tightened with fear. I wondered, *If I truly surrender all, what will the Lord demand from me? What will He take from me?* I was hesitant to let go and trust Him completely. I was afraid to follow.

My Designer slowly tore down my old perception grounded in fear and with great patience began building a new one. I struggled and agonized as He put each of my beliefs to the test. Did I just accept God's truth, or was I convinced?

The truth needed to move from my head to my heart as the rebuilding process continued. Job expressed it well. "I have heard of thee by the hearing of the ear: but now mine eye seeth thee" (Job 42:5).

One of the major factors that brought about my changed perspective was accepting the truth about the precious gifts we, as children of the Designer, are given. In this chapter we will talk about five of these gifts. Although we are given many more, these can significantly impact how we view our Designer and our relationship with Him. They can free us from so many lies that keep us in bondage.

They may not be new to you, but the critical question is, are they real to you? Have you accepted them as your own? Too often we give intellectual consent to God's truth, but we are not convinced of it in our hearts. Therefore, we continue to be plagued with doubt, worry, fear, and guilt.

Claiming the truth of the following five divine gifts and living in their reality will result in a spiritual freedom to serve from a heart of love. "If ye continue in my word, then are ye my disciples indeed; and ye shall know the truth, and the truth shall make you free" (John 8:31-32).

As you work through this chapter, take your time, pray, and ask your Designer to help you grasp these truths. Meditate (engage in contemplation or reflection) on them and claim them as your own.

DAY 1
UNCONDITIONAL LOVE

A husband and wife visited an orphanage where they hoped to adopt a child. In an interview with the boy they wanted, they told him in glowing terms about the many things they could give him. To their amazement, the little fellow said, "If you have nothing to offer except a good home, clothes, toys, and the other things that most kids have, I would just as soon stay here."

"What on earth could you want besides those things?" the woman asked.

"I just want someone to love me," replied the little boy.

Every heart needs love. But human love can turn cold and be lost, even with the best intentions and promises. When we open our hearts to love someone, and then, in time, they stop loving us, it is painful and can leave a gaping wound of rejection.

Our Designer does not love as people do. His love is pure, unchanging, eternal, and unconditional. Just think: Jesus, the One who designed and created you, truly loves you...not just the world in general but YOU! "Behold what manner of love the Father hath bestowed upon us, that we should be called the sons of God" (1 John 3:1).

Unconditional seems to be the one characteristic of our Designer's love that is especially difficult for us to comprehend.

The reason may be because human love is always conditional, and we are constantly needing to meet expectations.

Precisely what does the word *unconditional* mean? According to Webster's dictionary, the word means "not dependent on conditions, not limited, absolute." Synonyms for unconditional are "complete, pure: having no exceptions or restrictions."

A love that is unlimited and not dependent on conditions sounds too good to be true.

How do we know our Designer's love is unconditional?

Scripture tells us in 1 John 4:8 that God IS love. He does not just give love; He is the very essence of pure love. His love is never in response to an action; therefore, our behavior cannot affect it. "For I am persuaded that neither death, nor life, nor angels, nor principalities, nor powers, nor things present, nor things to come, nor height, nor depth, nor any other creature, shall be able to separate us from the love of God, which is in Christ Jesus our Lord" (Romans 8:38-39).

If our Lord always loves us, why do we sometimes feel unloved? This question has two possible answers. First, we are prone to judge things by our feelings, and nothing is more unstable than feelings. They can be affected by a comment, a look, a movie we watch, a book we read, or a song we hear. For women, we can be affected by changing hormone levels. Feelings frequently lie to us and are unreliable.

A wife whose husband is overseas in the military or away on a business trip may not always feel married. She has to handle day-to-day responsibilities on her own. She has to make decisions, run errands, supervise homework and science projects, dentist appointments, and a multitude of other daily family needs without her husband. To top it off, when she finally falls into bed at night, she is alone.

The distance between her and her husband does not, however, determine the reality of her marital status. Regardless of her emotions, she is still married.

Our Designer's truth is not based on or affected by our feelings. It is reliable and unchangeable. "If we believe not, yet he abideth faithful: he cannot deny himself" (2 Timothy 2:13).

Knowing our human weaknesses, the devil throws doubts or lies into our minds about God's Word and His promises. If we grab hold of these lies and mull them over in our minds, they will affect our emotions, creating negative feelings about our Designer's love.

The second reason we may not feel loved is unconfessed sin. When we sin, it interrupts our fellowship with our Designer. This interruption creates a sense of distance between us. If we repent and bring things quickly in order, our feelings of not being loved will dissipate.

If we continue in disobedience or we procrastinate getting things in order, however, the feelings of not being loved will grow. Like the married woman, our emotions may deny the truth. God has not changed, but our spiritual perception has. If our thoughts are not focused on God's truth, our view will be perverted.

I pray the reality of our Designer's unconditional love for you will sink deep into your heart. He loves you regardless of your past, your failures, or your weaknesses. He loves you just as you are. Claim this wonderful gift; rest in it; enjoy it. When it became a reality for me, I was deeply humbled and the sense of joy was incredible.

Dig Deeper:

- Do you struggle with feeling unloved by your Designer? If so, which of the reasons given above do you think could be the cause?
- How should we deal with known sin? (1 John 1:9)
- Read 1 John 4:9-10. Why did the Father send Jesus to die for you?
- Read Ephesians 2:4-5. Write out what this verse means to you.
- Write a letter to your Designer, expressing how you feel about His unconditional love for you.

My Thoughts:

_____

_____

_____

_____

_____

_____

_____

_____

_____

_____

_____

_____

_____

_____

_____

_____

DAY 2
GIFTS FROM OUR FATHER

According to Scripture, we become a child of God through faith in His Son and our Designer, Jesus Christ. "But as many as received him, to them gave he power to become the sons of God, even to them that believe on his name" (John 1:12).

When we accept Jesus as our Savior, a supernatural change occurs. "Therefore, if any man be in Christ, he is a new creature: old things are passed away; behold, all things are become new" (2 Corinthians 5:17).

We are the same person, and our circumstances have not changed. Our old sinful nature is not any different, so then we might ask what is new or what has changed?

The greatest change is that we are no longer separated from God but are now His children. We are spiritually alive and possess amazing, priceless, divine gifts.

One of these gifts is the indwelling Holy Spirit. "In whom ye also trusted, after that ye heard the word of truth, the gospel of your salvation, in whom also, after that ye believed, ye were sealed with that Holy Spirit of promise" (Ephesians 1:13). The Holy Spirit is God, and He will comfort, guide, teach, empower, and rebuke us, but He will never leave us.

Our spiritual life cannot be held in our hands or visibly seen and, therefore, can be challenging to grasp. In the same way, our new position as our Designer's child can be unclear. When we understand what this new position entails it will have a tremendous effect on our service for our Designer and our relationship with Him. But if we miss this we will think we have to earn the gifts we have already received.

When I understood my new position before the Father was secure in Christ and not dependent on me, I had a tremendous sense of relief and peace. It turned my relationship to my Designer around 180 degrees.

I have listed eight divine changes given to every believer in their position as a child of God. I pray that studying these truths will remove unnecessary pressure and guilt from your heart and bring joy and thanksgiving in their place. Write out the following verses.

- We are forgiven—Colossians 2:13-14
- We are reconciled (restored to harmony) to the Father—2 Corinthians 5:18
- We are redeemed (the price for our sins is paid)—1 Peter 1:18-19
- We are justified (made in right standing before the Father)—Romans 5:1
- We are sanctified (set apart for God's use)—1 Corinthians 6:11; Hebrews 10:10
- We are righteous (declared righteous or just before the Father)—Philippines 3:8-9; Isaiah 61:10
- We are accepted by the Father—Ephesians 1:8
- We are eternally secure—John 10:27-29; 1 John 6:13

Look at the verses you have written. What do they all have in common? The common denominator in all these changes is also the reason they are eternal, unchanging, and instantaneous. It is why they are NOT affected by anything we do or do not do! The common denominator is Jesus Christ. They are all based in and because of Jesus, the beloved Son of God and our Designer. They are GIVEN to us, NOT EARNED.

Dig Deeper:

- What does being a child of God mean to you?
- Read Ecclesiastes 3:14 and fill in the blanks. "I _____ that whatsoever God doeth, it shall be _____ ; _____ can be put to it, nor anything _____ from it: and God doeth it, that men should fear before him." How does this verse affect your position or standing before the Father?
- Read each of the eight points listed above again. How do you think living in their reality will affect your relationship with your Designer? How will it affect your service?
- To live in the reality of our new position, we must believe—trust—it is true. "Likewise reckon ye also yourselves to be dead indeed unto sin, but alive unto God through Jesus Christ our Lord" (Romans 6:11). If someone put a million dollars into your checking account and it was all correct and legal, you would be a millionaire. Just having it in the bank, however, would not change how you live. The only way to experience the benefits it can give you is to go to the bank, write your name on a withdrawal slip and claim the money.

Now write your name in the eight changes listed above, claim them as your own, thank your Designer for each one, and experience their benefit in your life. They were blood-bought.

My Thoughts:

_____

_____

_____

_____

_____
_____
_____
_____
_____
_____
_____
_____
_____
_____
_____
_____
_____
_____
_____
_____
_____
_____
_____
_____
_____
_____
_____
_____
_____
_____
_____
_____
_____
_____

_____

_____

_____

_____

_____

_____

_____

_____

_____

_____

_____

_____

_____

_____

_____

_____

_____

_____

_____

_____

_____

_____

_____

_____

_____

_____

_____

_____

DAY 3
UNLIMITED MERCY

"A missions student and pastor's wife expelled for cheating." These words could have appeared in the student paper and referred to me.

In our first year at Bible college my husband and I were required to take a class called Personal Evangelism. This class involved memorizing a multitude of Bible verses. At the end of the semester, the final exam consisted of writing out specific verses from memory. I had worked hard and spent numerous hours memorizing the required material and felt calm and confident as exam day arrived.

The room chosen for the test was a large auditorium with old-fashioned theater seats placed close together. There must have been about two hundred students present. We all took our seats. The test was passed out, and I began answering the questions. All was going well, and my confidence grew. Then it happened. A verse was required that I could not remember. Suddenly a surge of panic hit, and my stomach did a flip.

I frantically read through all the previous questions again in hopes of jarring my memory, but to no avail. My mind was racing. The answer was right on the tip of my tongue; yet it eluded me.

While my mind was working, my eyes drifted to my husband's paper. Immediately I saw the first word of the verse I was struggling with. I had it! In an instant the complete verse flashed into my mind. Momentary relief and elation flooded over me as I wrote down the verse. I finished the test and turned it in to the professor. My elation, however, was short-lived.

The test grades were posted. I received an A, both on the exam and for the course. I should have been thrilled, right? Wrong. I was miserable. I knew I did not deserve the A. I tried to justify my behavior, and, after all, no one knew what I had done—no one except the Lord and me, that is. The more I made excuses, the worse I felt. The Holy Spirit intensified His conviction until I could no longer resist.

With a heavy heart I decided to go to my professor and confess. Dr. W, the professor I had to talk with, was strict and not known for his mercy. He also had a position of authority and power over the students in his class. I was a nervous wreck when I arrived at his office. Upon entering, the secretary told me to go on in. I felt as if I were entering a den of lions and my heart would beat right out of my chest.

My professor looked up from his work as I walked in and asked what I wanted to talk to him about. Without a moment's hesitation my story spewed out of my mouth like soda from a shaken bottle.

When I finished, Dr. W looked back at his desk and didn't say a word. The following moments of silence felt like an eternity—an eternity that held my future in the balance. I could hear the seconds on the wall clock ticking loudly as the suspense in the room rose.

At last, Dr. W broke the silence. He looked up with a sober expression and said, "You know I could expel you from school for this."

"Yes, sir." I kept my eyes fixed on my trembling hands clasped in my lap.

Again, icy silence filled the air. Then he continued. "You will get an F for the test, and you must repeat the class."

I quickly agreed, and he dismissed me from his office. What a relief! Regardless of the discipline, I was just relieved it was over. The idea of taking the class again was not appealing. But it was so much better than being expelled from school, and I was thankful for the mercy my professor had shown me.

According to the dictionary, mercy is "clemency, leniency, and compassion, especially to an offender or one under your power." Simply put, mercy means not rendering all that an act or behavior deserves. My professor showed mercy to me as a student, but how many times does our Designer show mercy to us?

The gift of salvation comes out of God's mercy. "Not by works of righteousness which we have done, but according to his mercy he saved us" (Titus 3:5).

Every time we fail in our walk with Him and confess our sin, our Designer exercises mercy on our behalf. "But thou, O Lord, art a God full of compassion and gracious, longsuffering, and plenteous in mercy and truth" (Psalm 86:15).

We need to remember that mercy is a gift. It is not earned nor deserved by our good behavior. God's mercy is outrageous, beyond our understanding, and not reasonable. It is a supernatural, priceless gift from our loving Designer (Ephesians 2:4-5). Plus, the supply never runs out. "It is of the Lord's mercies that we are not consumed, because his compassions fail not. They are new every morning: great is thy faithfulness" (Lamentations 3:22-23).

Being convinced that our Designer is compassionate and merciful and that He cares about us makes it easier to come and confess our sins. I like the comment once made by Dr. David Jeremiah: "When we come to Him in true repentance, His mercy will just overflow us like waves of the sea, because He is rich in mercy."[6]

When I, despite my fear and trembling, went to my professor and confessed my act of cheating, I had no assurance he would be merciful. He was not required to show mercy.

But when we come before our Designer with a humble heart we can be assured of His mercy. We need have no fear; He will not withhold His mercy from His children, and we will not receive all that our actions deserve.

Mercy is an attribute, a part of our Designer's character. He is merciful just as He is love. Accept this wonderful gift from your Designer and rest in its truth. Remember: fear will have trouble growing in a heart assured of tender mercy.

Dig Deeper:

- How do we know our Designer will be compassionate with us? Read Psalm 103:13-14 and Hebrews 4:15 and write out your answer.
- How much mercy do we have? (Lamentations 3:22-23)
- Can you remember a time you were aware of your Designer's mercy?
- How does the reality of mercy affect your willingness to trust your Designer and follow His leading?

My Thoughts:

_____

_____

_____

_____

_____

_____

_____

_____

_____

DAY 4
AMAZING GRACE

How many times have you sung the song "Amazing Grace"? Did you know it is one of the best known and loved hymns of the last two decades and has been translated into sixty different languages? It has appeared on more than eleven thousand albums and is performed about ten million times annually. It is a popular song, and many people are singing about grace. But do they grasp the reality of what they are singing—do we?

Biblical grace is the unmerited favor of our Designer bestowed upon unworthy, undeserving humanity. It means we have what we could never obtain on our own. We experience grace because it pleases our Designer to give it to us. We do not deserve it; we cannot earn it. It is a marvelous, divine gift.

By grace we come to know Christ, we are forgiven, and we have eternal life. "For by grace are you saved through faith; and that not of yourselves: it is a gift of God" (Ephesians 2:8). Grace covers the life of a child of God from the beginning to the end.

The story of the prodigal son is a good illustration of grace. In the story we read how the younger son in a family demanded his inheritance, enabling him to leave home and enjoy life. "And the younger of them said to his father, Father, give me the portion of goods that falleth to me" (Luke 15:12).

His father granted him his wish, and the son left home full of expectations and dreams of adventure. "And not many days after the younger son gathered all together, and took his journey into a far country, and there wasted his substance with riotous living" (Luke 15:13).

But the high life turned to an empty life, and his dreams crashed on the rocks of reality. Things continued to decline until the young boy found himself without money or friends. A great famine covered the land, which intensified his situation. At last, when all options were gone, the young Jewish boy found himself in a filthy pig pen in search of food...a most degrading and repulsive situation. He could go no lower.

He was destitute and broken in spirit. There at the bottom he remembered home. His mind flooded with memories of his loving father, and he realized he had only one answer, one hope. He had to go back home.

What the father had been doing while the son was away is especially meaningful to me. "But when he was yet a long way off, his father saw him" (Luke 15:20). The father had not forgotten or given up on his young son. He had not stopped loving his son. He was there every day waiting, expecting him to come back home.

Now the story gets even better. "His father saw him, and had compassion, and ran and fell on his neck and kissed him" (Luke 15:20).

Can you imagine the joy and relief of the father when he saw his son? After long days of not knowing where his dear son was or even if he was still alive, the father suddenly sees him in the distance.

Overcome with joy and excitement, tears filling his eyes, the father runs to meet his long-lost son. He could hardly wait to wrap his arms around his son's neck, kiss him, and hold him tight. It did not matter that the boy was ragged and probably smelled of the pig pen. It did not matter that he had spent all his inheritance and lived an ungodly, immoral life. All that was important was that his wayward son was back home. What a beautiful picture of amazing grace.

The son, although happy to see the father, wanted most of all to make things right. He was quick to confess his sin and unworthiness. He did not make excuses for his behavior, nor did he blame his father, his brothers, or his ex-friends in the city. He repented, taking responsibility for his decisions and behavior. "And the son said unto him, Father, I have sinned against heaven, and in thy sight, and am no more worthy to be called thy son" (Luke 15:20). The result was reconciliation.

While I was stumbling around in my depression, I became angry at my Designer and began to rebel. I felt my situation was unfair and undeserved. I decided that if my Designer treated me like this, I did not want to serve Him. My behavior and my thought life were anything but godly. I yielded to temptations and justified my actions. My Designer let me choose, just like the father in our story above let his young son choose.

Like the prodigal son, life did not go well for me. I began to miss what I had when my relationship with my Designer was in order. I missed peace and joy. Self-indulgence and self-will had brought only pain, regret, guilt, and distress. None of my reasoning could quiet the still small voice inside my heart, calling me to repent.

After feeling hopeless and playing with thoughts of suicide, my situation was clear. I came to the end of myself; my pride crushed, I had to get things right with my Designer and go back home.

With a broken heart I humbly confessed my sin. I admitted my arrogant, rebellious behavior and asked for forgiveness. Words cannot describe the soothing peace I experienced as my Designer's grace flowed over me. "If we confess our sins, He is faithful and just to forgive us our sins, and to cleanse us from all our unrighteousness" (1 John 1:9).

In the prodigal son's story, we read how, despite the son's behavior and his wrongdoing, his father not only forgave him but restored all that confirmed his position as a son. "But the father said to his servants, Bring forth the best robe, and put it on him; and put a ring on his hand, and shoes on his feet; and bring hither the fatted calf, and kill it; and let us eat, and be merry" (Luke 15:22-23).

When we repent and confess our sin, harmonious fellowship with our Designer will be restored. We can once again enjoy our position as His child.

This chapter has talked about our Designer's unconditional love, our new position before our Father, mercy, and grace. All of these gifts are independent of our works, obedience, or worthiness. They are GIFTS.

Dig Deeper:

- How does the truth about grace make you feel about your relationship with your Designer?
- Have you drifted away from "home"? Don't be afraid to come back to your Father. He is waiting for you. Confess your sin and let Him restore you into sweet fellowship. The Designer's grace is there for you.
- In what situations have you experienced God's amazing grace?
- How can the reality of God's grace influence your willingness to serve Him?

My Thoughts:

_____

_____

_____

_____

_____

_____

_____

_____

_____

_____

_____

_____

_____

_____

_____

_____

_____

_____

_____

_____

_____

_____

_____

_____

_____

_____

_____

_____

_____

_____

_____

_____

_____

DAY 5
ENDURING PATIENCE

We want what we want, and we want it now. Society seeks instant gratification and does not like to wait for anything. Immediate messaging, instant news, and thousands of apps enabling us to view the world on demand fuel man's impatience.

We want quick answers to complex problems, diets to evaporate pounds overnight, steps to happy relationships that require no time or effort and to know if we are pregnant the morning after. We want to be spiritual giants without surrender. We want to understand what our Designer is doing without spending time with Him. But instant and immediate are not words that often describe how our Designer works.

Let us consider Noah. He worked on the ark 120 years. I am sure God could have enabled Noah to accomplish this project in less time if He had wanted to. It did not need to take so long, so why the delay? "When once the longsuffering of God waited in the days of Noah, while the ark was a preparing" (1 Peter 3:20). The delay had a purpose. God was patient and giving humanity more time to repent and be saved.

How long did it take you to answer the Holy Spirit's convicting call and accept Christ as your Savior? Few people respond the first time they sense conviction. What if our Designer had no patience and was not willing to call again, and again, and again? "The Lord is not slack concerning his promise, as some men count slackness; but is longsuffering to us-ward, not willing that any should perish, but that all should come to repentance" (2 Peter 3:9).

Our Designer does not tire of teaching us His truth. As we read His Word and meditate on it, the Holy Spirit brings understanding. Grasping God's Word does not happen overnight. It is a process and takes time. "For precept must be upon precept, precept upon precept; line upon line, line upon line; here a little, and there a little" (Isaiah 28:10).

New believers like babies need milk regularly to grow. "As newborn babes, desire the sincere milk of the word, that ye may grow thereby" (1 Peter 2:2). How long we remain a spiritual baby is up to us.

Our Designer patiently orchestrates situations and circumstances to grow our faith and draw us closer to Him. He patiently teaches us our need for Him and the insufficiency of our strength. It takes time for the Holy Spirit to reveal the lies stored in our subconscious, our worldly thoughts, motives, attitudes, and values. I am so thankful He does not give up when we don't see it right away. He remains faithful and persistent.

The Bible contains many examples of our Designer's patience. One, in particular, is Moses. Moved by the cruel treatment of his fellow Israelites, he wanted to help them. His first attempts were according to his reasoning, however, and not in God's way or timing. They backfired and did not bring about the desired results. The Designer wanted to use Moses to help the Israelites, but first he needed to be humbled, molded, and changed. His training ground was the desert where he would spend forty years.

During those years, Moses may have forgotten all about the Israelites' situation. He may have thought they had nothing more to do with his life, but his Designer had not forgotten. On the contrary, his Designer had been patiently training and preparing Moses to accomplish His purpose.

As I mentioned in the introduction, I sincerely wanted to serve my Designer and had tried hard to do so; but when we resigned as missionaries, I was sure my service was over. I believed the Lord was through with me. I felt as if I were on the backside of a desert.

Like Moses, I needed to be humbled, taught, disciplined, and changed. I needed to understand my Designer did not want my efforts; He wanted my heart. He wanted a surrendered will. I am incredibly thankful our Designer is not like men but is patient and faithful. He did not give up on me, and He won't give up on you either.

Dig Deeper:
- Have you had a dream fall apart? What did you learn from this experience?
- Do you feel as if your Designer has forgotten about you? Why?

Can you think of times when your Designer was longsuffering and patient with you?

We have seen our Designer's power, authority, and individual care in designing each of us. We have also learned more about His unconditional love, divine gifts in salvation, mercy, grace, and patience.
- How have these truths affected your willingness to trust your Designer? "Trust in the Lord with all your heart; and lean not unto your own understanding" (Proverbs 3:5).

My Thoughts:

_____

_____

_____

_____

_____

_____

_____

_____
_____
_____
_____
_____
_____
_____
_____
_____
_____
_____
_____
_____
_____
_____
_____
_____
_____
_____
_____
_____
_____
_____
_____
_____
_____
_____
_____
_____
_____
_____
_____

Chapter Three
PUTTING THE PIECES TOGETHER

What about the pieces in our puzzle? What are they, how do we get the right ones, and how do we know when and where to place them? The pieces are the people, relationships, experiences, achievements, failures, difficulties, events, and challenges we encounter. In short, they are what we experience every day.

Although many pieces are out of our control, they are never an accident or without our Designer's permission. Remember, He is all-powerful, all-knowing, and the supreme ruler over heaven and earth. He has a purpose and place for every piece that enters our life puzzle. "I will cry unto God most high; unto God that performeth all things for me" (Psalm 57:2).

DAY 1
SIZE, SHAPE, AND COLOR OF THE PIECES

The pieces of a puzzle can vary in size and shape, with different shades of color to give them depth and contrast. Some pieces are dark or black, while others are bright and shades of white. Each piece alone provides little indication of how the puzzle will look when completed.

Similarly, the pieces in our life puzzles also vary in size, shape, and color. We enjoy the light, bright pieces that bring peace, joy, and blessings. In our opinion, all the pieces could be light and bright. Our Designer knows we need depth, however, and that requires the dark shades.

An interesting thing about the pieces is what looks small and insignificant can dramatically impact our lives. In the Gospel of John, we read about two little fish a mother packed in the lunch of her young son, never suspecting they would become part of a miracle to feed more than five thousand people. I am sure that little boy never again looked at a fish without recalling that miraculous event.

In our lives the little piece may be a warm hug when we are discouraged or a helping hand when we are about to go under; it may be an unexpected phone call or the persistent visiting of a pastor. It may be a friend who is willing to listen. Our Designer knows what we need, and He will bring the needed pieces into our puzzle. "Your Father knoweth what things ye have need of before ye ask him" (Matthew 6:8).

The dark piece may be a problem we can't solve or a job we have no strength to do. Our Designer may give us an autistic child or entrust us with the care of aging parents. These kinds of pieces show us our dependence. "God does not ask us to do the things that are naturally easy for us—He only asks us to do the things we are perfectly fit to do through His grace" (Oswald Chambers).[7]

Some are unlovable pieces. These are the unthankful, inconsiderate, unkind people we have to deal with regularly, such as a boss, co-worker, neighbor, or even a relative. We want the Lord to move these pieces out of our lives or change them, but He doesn't. Instead, He wants us to learn to draw on His love and do what seems impossible. "I can do all things through Christ which strengtheneth me" (Philippians 4:13).

Rough, jagged pieces are designed to teach us forgiveness. I have talked to people who have been abused as children, been raped, lost their child to murder, been lied about, and suffered traumatic loss due to someone's negligence. Sadly, many times the one causing the pain never accepted responsibility for their actions. In every case, though, regardless of how hard it was, forgiveness brought them great peace and relief, and their relationship with their Designer deepened.

The rough, jagged pieces have an essential place in our puzzles. They allow us to experience our Designer's tender comfort and compassion. He feels our pain, and He understands. He wants to draw us close and remind us each piece has a purpose in His loving plan. One day it will all make sense, but for now we have to trust Him. "For I know the thoughts that I think toward you, saith the Lord, thoughts of peace, and not of evil, to give you an expected end" (Jeremiah 29:11).

Then we see those bright, light-colored pieces I mentioned earlier. Our Designer knows when we need success and accomplishment. He knows when to send the pay raise at work, the unexpected phone call bearing good news, or that long-awaited answer to our prayer. Good and joyful pieces such as these are not due to our planning and ability. Our Designer arranges them.

"Every good gift and every perfect gift is from above, and cometh down from the Father of lights, with whom is no variableness, neither shadow of turning" (James 1:17).

Dig Deeper:
- What small things have you experienced that made a big difference in your life?
- What have you learned from difficult pieces?
- What unexpected pieces have brought you joy and blessing?
- Which pieces do you struggle with the most? What do you think your Designer wants to teach you?

My Thoughts:

_____

_____

_____

_____

_____

_____

_____

_____

_____

_____

_____

_____

_____

_____

_____

_____

DAY 2
THE TIMING OF THE PIECES

An Olympics trainer once said that timing is everything. Timing is essential, and our society gears us for FAST. Modern technology is continually developing new items to help us accomplish work faster. Unconsciously, we may move this mind-set to our Designer.

We want our needs met, answers to our prayers, and changes in our circumstances to take place immediately. Young people get impatient waiting for that perfect one to come into their lives, while married couples are often disappointed and discouraged waiting for their first baby.

We get impatient waiting for a job, the desired opportunity, lost loved ones to be saved or improved health.

Underneath these expectations is our human desire for control and our pride. We think we know the best timing, and we set expectations for our Designer. We forget the purpose of our life. It is not about us, but it is for His glory. We were created for our Designer. He was not created for us.

Our Designer is aware of our impatience, but He does not hurry. He does not run on our schedule. Many stories in the Bible reveal this fact, and Lazarus's story is one of them.

The Designer loved Lazarus, and when He heard Lazarus was sick we would expect Him to come to his aid quickly, but He did not. "When he had heard therefore that he was sick, he abode two days still in the same place where he was" (John 11:6).

Lazarus's Designer did just the opposite of what we might expect. He waited until Lazarus died before arriving on the scene. His timing does not seem reasonable to us, nor did it to Mary and

Martha. Maybe this is because our focus is on the moment and what we judge as important.

Our Designer is not only focused on the now, but also on what He is working for eternity. He is focused not only on the visible but on the invisible.

When the Designer did arrive at the home of Lazarus, He answered the "if only" remarks from Mary and Martha by reminding them that He was the resurrection and the life. They thought He was referring to the resurrection in the future when He was referring to the present.

We can read the story and learn how the Designer raised Lazarus from the dead, which was the Designer's plan from the beginning. Undoubtedly, the time of waiting brought about a miracle that significantly impacted the people. His timing was perfect.

When our Designer brings waiting time into our life, we often struggle. We struggle because we cannot see what God is doing. It feels as if nothing is happening or maybe our Designer is not going to answer or is not interested in our needs.

We are like the young child who planted some flower seeds and went out every day anxious to see the flowers growing. The first few days she saw nothing. She would go back inside sad and discouraged because she could not see any change.

After a few days she was so frustrated and in such doubt that she dug up the seeds. To her surprise, small hair-like roots were growing, drawing nourishment from the soil and preparing the little plant to burst through the earth. The young child realized that just because she could not see the change did not mean growth was not taking place. Our Designer is always working and has a purpose when He puts us in His waiting room.

For several years my mother desired a second child, but she did not get pregnant. Then when she was in her middle thirties her gynecologist told her she could not have any more children. In the process of time, my father also chose to have a vasectomy. Another child was no longer an option, and I grew up alone.

Our Designer, however, had a different plan in mind. In the early spring of 1967, my parents bought a little farm. My mother quit her job with the school district and enjoyed being at home, cooking and entertaining.

During this time, my mother's menstrual cycle became irregular. She called her doctor about it, and he assured her it was not unusual at her age. She was forty at the time. My mother began to put on weight. She insisted the extra cooking and baking she was doing was to blame.

Her belly grew and she began experiencing abdominal disturbance which she described as terrible gas. It became a real concern to my dad, and he insisted she visit her doctor.

After examining my mother and taking an X-ray, the doctor informed her that she was six months' pregnant with her second child. To say my parents were shocked by this news would have been an understatement.

I was now twenty-one, married, and living in another state. I remember calling my mom on a Saturday morning, as I usually did, and hearing her ask, "Honey, do you want a brother or a sister?" Now my parents were not the only ones shocked. Crazy timing from our perspective, but perfect timing in the scheme of events our Designer knew lay ahead.

My sister brought much joy to my parents. She helped fill the empty spot created when my husband and I left for the mission field. My sister and I are now both grandmothers, and I realize she was a unique piece not only in the life puzzle of my parents but also in mine. His timing was perfect.

The timing of the various pieces in our life puzzle is our Designer's responsibility. Realizing our limited knowledge of the future, the needs in others' hearts, or our Designer's plan will make it easier for us to surrender our expectations on timing. "A man's heart deviseth his way: but the Lord directeth his steps" (Proverbs 16:9).

Based on what we know of our Designer's nature and His care for each of us, we can rest in confidence that His timing, including the periods of waiting, will be for our best. Trusting will relieve much worry and stress. "Trust in the Lord with all your heart; and lean not unto your own understanding" (Proverbs 3:5).

Dig Deeper:
- Make a list of the times your Designer's timing was different from what you wanted.
- What differences did His timing make?
- Read the following verses. What do they say about waiting on the Lord? Psalm 27:14, 33:20-22, 39:7; Lamentations 3:24-26; Micah 7:7; Isaiah 40:31
- How do you feel when your Designer does not work according to your expectations? What do you think is the reason for your feelings?
- Why is it important to let your Designer control the timing of the pieces in your life puzzle?

My Thoughts:

_____

_____

_____

_____

_____

_____

_____

_____

_____

_____

_____

_____

_____

_____

_____

_____

_____

_____

_____

_____

_____

_____

_____

_____

_____

_____

_____

_____

_____

_____

_____

_____

DAY 3
THE SIZE OF OUR PUZZLE

Not all puzzles are the same size. Some have four or five large pieces, while others have a hundred. Then there are the giant ones with ten thousand pieces. Naturally, the smaller the puzzle, the less time it takes to complete.

Our life puzzles also vary in size, and our Designer does not tell us in advance how many pieces they will have or how long it will take until all the pieces are in place. David tells us that our Designer already knows these answers while we are in our mother's womb. "I will praise thee; for I am fearfully and wonderfully made: marvellous are thy works; and that my soul knoweth right well. Thine eyes did see my substance, yet being imperfect; and in thy book all my members were written, which in continuance were fashioned, when as yet there was none of them" (Psalm 139:14, 16).

When a baby is born, we expect a long life—a puzzle with many pieces; but the Designer does not promise this. "Boast not thyself of tomorrow; for thou knowest not what a day may bring forth" (Proverbs 27:1).

John the Baptist was a special son. He was the answer to a long-time prayer of Zacharias and Elisabeth. So much time had elapsed that they had given up on receiving an answer. Then one day the angel Gabriel stood before Zacharias and informed him the time had come and they would have a son.

No doubt Zacharias and Elisabeth hoped their son would live a long life for the Lord. But their son John, a chosen servant of Christ, lived only about thirty-three years and was then brutally murdered at an ungodly woman's request. Was his death premature?

John preached and prepared the way for Jesus, the Messiah. Although his life ended too soon from our perspective, he fulfilled his designed purpose. Since we have no idea of the designed purpose behind anyone's life, not even our own, we cannot know the time needed for its completion.

Jesus lived for only thirty-three years. Just think of all the people He could have healed, all the lost who would have accepted Him as their Savior, all the teaching He could have done if He had lived longer. Do we not consider thirty-three years a short life?

Nevertheless, Jesus made this declaration to His Father. "I have glorified thee on earth: I have finished the work which thou gavest me to do" (John 17:4). Jesus' puzzle was complete after thirty-three years because He had fulfilled the will of His Father.

In 2012 my husband was in the hospital suffering from peritonitis (a severe inflammation of the abdominal lining). The doctors said they had no hope for his recovery. But three months and twenty-four surgeries later he came home, and within six months you could not tell he had ever been sick.

Some dear friends of ours had three daughters and greatly desired a son. After much prayer and many years of waiting, the answer came, and little Jimmy was born. His parents and sisters were thrilled with this long-awaited piece the Designer placed in their lives.

One Thursday when Jimmy was about a year old, he became ill. His parents were not alarmed since the other children had all been sick earlier in the week. But Jimmy's condition grew rapidly worse. They took him to the hospital on Saturday, and the following Monday Jimmy's Designer took him home.

What happened? Did his Designer lose control? Was Jimmy taken too soon? No, little Jimmy accomplished what the Designer planned. He had given his family great joy and unforgettable memories, and he is now waiting for them in heaven. Jimmy's life did not go according to his parents' plan, but it went according to the one who designed him—the one who is in control of all things. "All power is given unto me in heaven and in earth" (Matthew 28:18).

Why do adults live and children die? We do not know the answer, and we have trouble understanding it. It will help if we remember life is not about us, but about what our Designer's plan is and what brings Him glory.

Both of the above stories resulted in people accepting Christ as their Savior and Christians growing closer to Him. We need to be careful about making assumptions and setting expectations about life. "Whereas ye know not what shall be on the morrow. For what is your life? It is even a vapour that appeareth for a little time, and then vanisheth away. For that ye ought to say, If the Lord will, we shall live, and do this, or that" (James 4:14-15).

Job lost all his possessions, his wealth, and his children on the same day. How did Job respond to this tremendous loss? "The Lord gave, and the Lord hath taken away; blessed be the name of the Lord" (Job 1:21).

We will not always understand our Designer's plan, and we may not like it. We may argue with Him or even get angry. Remember His great love for us and what He has said. "For my thoughts are not your thoughts, neither are your ways my ways, saith the Lord. For as the heavens are higher than the earth, so are my ways higher than your ways, and my thoughts than your thoughts" (Isaiah 55:8-9).

Our Designer is almighty God and knows the end from the beginning. "I am God, and there is none like me, declaring the end from the beginning, and from ancient times the things that are not yet done, saying, My counsel shall stand, and I will do all my pleasure" (Isaiah 46:9-10).

He does all things well, including the things we do not understand. We will only find the peace and strength we need when we choose to trust Him based on what we know about Him.

Faith is the evidence of trusting a God we cannot see. It is resting in the assurance that our Designer knows and does what is best for us, regardless of how it may appear.

Dig Deeper:

- Do you find yourself making assumptions about the length of your life or the lives of your family?
- Does our Designer care about the sadness and grief we experience? 1 Peter 5:7, Psalm 34:18
- Where is our source of comfort? 2 Corinthians 1:3-4; Isaiah 41:10
- Why is it vital for us to accept His timing?
- Do you believe your Designer does have power over all things and is always in control? What do you base your answer on?

My Thoughts:

_____

_____

_____

_____

_____

_____

_____

_____

DAY 4
MOLDED TO FIT ANOTHER PUZZLE

Just as the people we encounter are pieces in our puzzle, each of us is a designed piece in someone else's puzzle. We influence and play a part in the lives of those around us. Sometimes our influence can affect generations to come.

Jesus said, "He who believes in me…out of his heart will flow rivers of living water" (John 7:38). What flows out of our lives affects others.

As we yield control to our Designer and follow His leading, His living water will flow through us and be a blessing to those around us, even to our children and grandchildren. Regardless of how little the visible effects of our lives may appear, they are essential and our Designer has planned them. "God rarely allows a person to see how great a blessing he is to others" (Oswald Chambers).[8]

The water of a river affects places far from its source. When a stream from a lake waters a field, plants grow. As the plants grow, the fruit develops and is picked, packaged, and shipped to stores around the country. You and I go to the store and buy the fruit grown in a field watered by a stream running from the lake. The fruit helps us grow and maintain our health, which allows us to impact the lives of others by serving and loving them. We may not even be aware of the lake that supplied the first needed water, but it played an essential part in enabling us to serve others today.

My grandmother was a simple country woman and did not have the opportunity for much education. I'm not sure she could even read, but she loved the Lord and had a burden for her family. My parents were not interested in church, though. As a result, my grandmother picked me up every Sunday and took me to Sunday school.

At the age of ten, I accepted Christ as my Savior. Although my parents were still not interested in the things of the Lord, I continued to attend church and grew spiritually.

In my Designer's timing I married my husband, and God called us to be missionaries. Through our fifty-three years of full-time ministry, many have come to know the Lord, churches have started, and believers have been trained to carry the living water to lands where we cannot go. Thus, my grandmother's influence has contributed to my impact on others.

Paul wrote this to Timothy: "When I call to remembrance the unfeigned faith that is in thee, which dwelt first in thy grandmother Lois, and in thy mother Eunice; and I am persuaded that in thee also" (2 Timothy 1:5). According to our Designer's plan, Timothy grew in faith and became a pastor of New Testament churches.

Our Designer is continually forming us to fit into the life puzzles around us. My experience with depression gives me the ability to relate to others struggling with this issue. Our friends who lost their little boy can minister to parents going through this heartache much better than I can because their loss formed them to be that piece.

The piece we are in another puzzle may be small: a kind deed, an encouraging word, a prepared meal, or a hospital visit. It could be more significant such as being a wife, mom, grandmother, sister, best friend, pastor's wife, teacher, caregiver, ministry leader, or counselor.

All pieces are needed to complete the whole.

It is not up to us to choose the piece we will be in another puzzle. "God places his saints where they will bring Him the most glory, and we are totally incapable of judging where that may be" (Oswald Chambers).[9] We need to leave the choice up to our Designer. He alone knows where we fit the best.

One day my husband and I were working on a five-hundred-piece puzzle. One section consisted of small, green pieces of various shades. It was challenging to find just the right one to fit in any one space. One morning I noticed that section of the puzzle appeared finished, and my husband looked quite pleased with himself. After taking a closer look, however, some of the green pieces did not fit. He had just forced them together. Sometimes we try to do this in life.

We try to force a relationship, a job position, a ministry idea, or some other situation we desire. If we continue in this way, we can cause friction and pain to ourselves and others. Sometimes the consequences of such a forced action can last a lifetime.

When we demand or try to force things to go our way, our Designer's living water is not flowing through us, but rather the polluted water of self-will and pride.

We will have more peace and less stress and grief if we will yield and relinquish the control to our Designer. We can trust Him to put us where He has designed us to fit the best. "God always gives the best to those who leave the choice with him" (Jim Elliot).[10]

Dig Deeper:

- Why do you think God often does not let us know how much we are a blessing to others?
- Can you think of people who have been a particular blessing to you? How did they influence your life?
- Have you ever tried to force something that was not the will of your Designer? How did that work out?
- What are the benefits of letting our Designer direct our relationships?

- What have you experienced that fits you to be that designed piece for someone else's life puzzle?

My Thoughts:

_____

_____

_____

_____

_____

_____

_____

_____

_____

_____

_____

_____

_____

_____

_____

_____

_____

_____

_____

_____

_____

_____

_____

_____

_____

_____

_____

_____

_____

_____

_____

_____

_____

_____

_____

_____

_____

_____

_____

_____

_____

_____

_____

_____

_____

_____

_____

_____

_____

_____

_____

_____

DAY 5
DIVINE ADVANCE PREPARATION

Have you ever anticipated a problem in the future and worried about how you would deal with it? The women going to the tomb where Christ was buried did exactly that.

Early in the morning on the first day of the week, Mary Magdalene and Mary, the mother of James, and Salome were on their way to the tomb with spices to anoint the body of Jesus. "And they said among themselves, Who shall roll us away the stone from the door of the sepulcher?" (Luke 16:3). They were anticipating a problem.

It is not uncommon for us to be anxious about the future. We hesitate to go through an unexpected door of opportunity, to take on a new responsibility, or to go through the medical test the doctor has ordered. We hesitate to go where we have not been before, often because we, like the two women in Luke 16, anticipate a problem.

We don't know and can't say how things will turn out, and that is precisely the point. We don't see the future. Our Designer, on the other hand, does. In fact, He knows everything about us, past, present, and future.

"Remember the former things of old: for I am God. And there is none else: I am God, and there is none like me, declaring the end from the beginning, and from ancient times the things that are not yet done, saying, My counsel shall stand, and I will do all my pleasure" (Isaiah 46:9-10). Our Designer is all-knowing.

When the women arrived at the tomb, "They saw the stone was rolled away: for it was very great" (Mark 16:4). The problem they anticipated was solved before they arrived.

One day God gave Joseph a dream regarding the future. He dreamed his eleven older brothers and his father would bow before him. At that time, no one could imagine how or why such a thing would happen, but the Designer's plan was already in place.

Time and the unexpected would be required to fulfill this dream. It looked for a while like Joseph's vision didn't have a chance of becoming a reality. But Joseph's Designer knew precisely the time frame of events and what pieces were needed not only in Joseph's puzzle but also in the life puzzles of each of his family members.

The Designer sent the Midianite merchants by just at the moment Joseph's brothers wanted to dispose of him. It was the Designer who blessed Joseph and gave him favor in the house of the Egyptian. "And the Lord was with Joseph, and he was a prosperous man; and he was in the house of his master the Egyptian. And his master saw that the Lord was with him, and that the Lord made all that he did to prosper in his hand" (Genesis 39:2-3).

The Designer orchestrated the drought and famine that forced Joseph's family to Egypt and reunited him with his family. Not only was there a family reunion, but it also brought about the fulfillment of Joseph's dream.

When his brothers realized who Joseph had become, second in authority to the pharaoh of Egypt, they were afraid; but Joseph had grown wise. "And God sent me before you to preserve you a posterity in the earth, and to save your lives by a great deliverance. So now it was not you that sent me hither, but God" (Genesis 45:7-8). Now Joseph saw that the events of his life were not mere accidents or coincidence, but rather all according to his Designer's plan.

Every piece in Joseph's puzzle—including the hard, painful, disappointing ones he could not understand and which seemed unfair—was necessary to accomplish his Designer's purpose. Every step divinely arranged.

When we first arrived in Germany, it was a strange feeling. Since we had never been here before, we did not know anyone, nor could we speak the language. We had definitely stepped into the unknown.

During our preparation time we had written to a missionary living in Germany, and he had given us some factual information. We were anxious to meet him and his family. But after meeting them we learned they were planning to leave the country. Needless to say, we were disappointed. The missionary did help us with our government paperwork and with finding an apartment in the city where we wanted to attend language school.

I remember the night he took us to a little store, right as it was closing, to get a few groceries. Then he dropped us off at our new apartment and said, "God bless you," and drove away. There we were in a strange land and couldn't speak a word of the language. The feeling of being alone swept over us, and our minds filled with anticipated problems. What now? What if we could not get into language school? How would we start? What do we do next?

Our sovereign Designer had already gone before and prepared the way for us. It turned out a woman in our apartment house had been married to an Englishman—she spoke English and was a tremendous help.

Then we needed someone to watch our two young children while we attended language school. Remember: we did not know anyone here. A family in our building had a teenage son who was learning English in school, and he befriended us. His mother heard of our need and volunteered to watch our children. Again, answers to our needs prepared in advance.

The language class we needed was full—until two people did not show up for the course. Their places became ours. Stepping out into the future, into the unknown, may be scary, but it is safe when you are in fellowship with your Designer and following Him. "And the Lord, he it is that doth go before thee; he will be with thee, he will not fail thee, neither forsake thee: fear not, neither be dismayed" (Deuteronomy 31:8).

Our Designer is sovereign, all-powerful, all-knowing, and personally interested in each of us. All we need to do is follow His leading. "The Lord is my shepherd...he leadeth me" (Psalm 23:1a, 2b).

"Don't be afraid of tomorrow; God is already there." — Unknown

Dig Deeper:

- What unknowns cause you anxiety? How can accepting your position as God's child help you?
- How do you think your Designer wants you to view the future?
- List all the ways that anxiety and worry can eliminate unknown difficulties.
- Make a list of all the situations in the future that concern you. Now lay them before your Designer and ask Him to help you turn loose and trust Him wo work. Find Bible verses to help you.

My Thoughts:

_____

_____

_____

_____

_____

_____

Chapter Four
DANGER: TRAPS AND PITFALLS

While our life's puzzle is coming together, we are also engaged in a spiritual war with a powerful, cunning, and ruthless enemy. Satan and his angels are always busy setting traps and placing pitfalls in our way. "For we wrestle not against flesh and blood, but against principalities, against powers, against the rulers of the darkness of this world, against spiritual wickedness in high places" (Ephesians 6:12).

Being made aware and forewarned of some of these dangers can help us avoid them. "Be sober, be vigilant; because your adversary the devil, as a roaring lion, walketh about seeking whom he may devour" (1 Peter 5:8).

Our enemy observes five essential factors in setting his traps.

- He knows human nature. Satan is well acquainted with how we tick. He has been watching and studying us since Adam and Eve. While society, technology, values, culture, and governments have changed, man's human nature has not.

- He knows our likes, dislikes, and weaknesses. No doubt, by simple observation, Satan knows our preferences and desires. He sees what we work for, what disappoints us, what we get upset about, and what we spend our time, energy, and money on. He knows what will tempt us.

- He knows the right bait and the right time. When I was a child, I often went fishing with my dad. He especially enjoyed fishing for Kokanee salmon in the mountain lakes of Colorado. I learned that when the salmon were hungry, nightcrawlers—big, fat worms—were the best bait.

  Satan knows when we are hungry and dissatisfied. We may hunger for someone to listen to us, to make us feel special. We may desire recognition, money, or position. Whatever our appetite is craving, our enemy knows just the right bait and will bring it by when we are the weakest and least prepared. "But every man is tempted, when he is drawn away of his own lust and enticed" (James 1:14).

- He waits until we are comfortable before closing the trap. We dabble in sin just a little, and nothing significant happens. We begin neglecting our Bible reading and make little time to pray. Life still seems to go along okay.

  We are extra friendly with the neighbor and maybe even meet for a cup of coffee. We join an online chat group with nothing evil in mind. We are just enjoying interacting with other people. We become comfortable and relaxed, unaware of the enemy's subtle working. Then suddenly the trap slams shut! We could find ourselves caught in an affair or some other undesirable situation.

DAY 1
GUILT VERSUS CONVICTION

"Remember what you did? How can you call yourself a Christian? God can't use someone with your past."

Have you ever had thoughts such as these enter your thinking? In the Book of Revelation, Satan is called the accuser of the saints. He does not only accuse us before God, but he loves to whisper accusations in our ears. He reminds us of our past sins and failures. His purpose is to draw us away from our Designer by playing on our feelings of fear: fear of disapproval, consequences, or punishment.

When this happens, it feels as if a dense, black cloud moves in from the outside and settles over us, obscuring the Light. We may not know why we are feeling guilty, but it can be paralyzing.

It can cause us to feel defeated and unaccepted by our Designer and often includes feelings of shame and dread. Close behind come feelings of discouragement, loss of incentive, and depression. Our thoughts turn inward centering on ourselves and all that is not going right in our lives.

I can remember as a young missionary wife, getting on my knees with tears rolling down my face pleading with God not to be angry with me. I was not convicted of any particular sin, but under major attack from the accuser. All I could see were my failures and weaknesses.

Self-centered thinking excludes the Designer from our thoughts. We are no longer in fellowship with our Designer or thinking about His Word, but rather centered on self, what we want, and what we do not have.

When we get caught in this trap, our old nature takes over, and we start listening to the father of lies and ignoring the truths of our Designer. Lies always lead to wrong emotions and wrong actions.

One reason the trap can be so effective is that we may be confused about guilt and conviction. In our natural state we are all sinners and stand guilty and condemned before a holy God. "For all have sinned, and come short of the glory of God" (Romans 3:23).

This guilt can only be dealt with by the blood of Christ. Once we have accepted Him as our Savior, we no longer stand guilty before the Father but are washed clean, justified, and forgiven. "Being justified freely by his grace through the redemption that is in Christ Jesus" (Romans 3:24). We are now free of condemnation. "There is therefore now no condemnation to them which are in Christ Jesus" (Romans 8:1).

Our enemy brings on guilty feelings that are based on a lie and not the truth. These feelings should not be confused with conviction from the Holy Spirit. The word *conviction* means "to convince someone of the truth; to reprove."

When we disobey our Designer, it does not change our position as His child, but it does cause a break or strain in our fellowship with Him. Because our Designer loves us and wants our fellowship, He cannot leave us in this state. The Holy Spirit begins to work, and by His convicting power, He will reveal our sin and work to bring us to repentance.

Repentance is more than a guilty conscience, feeling sorry for the deed, or feeling remorse about the possible consequences. It recognizes that our sin grieves our Designer and indicates a change of mind. We choose to turn from what was sin and turn to what is right. Conviction is a work of love and meant to bring about restoration and blessing.

The next time you experience feelings of guilt, proof them. Is there a definite conviction of sin? If so, then confess it, turn from it, and accept your Designer's forgiveness.

Is it the enemy trying to catch you in his guilt trap? If this is the case, here is how to escape it: submit to your Designer's authority and acknowledge Him as your Lord. Admit the sin the enemy refers to and remind him it is all under your Designer's blood and forgiven. Resist the accusation by refusing to think about that sin or event anymore. The enemy will flee (James 4:7).

These steps may sound easy, even too easy to be effective, but they are powerful and will work because they are biblical. Satan has no power against our Designer.

Dig Deeper:

- What things cause you to feel guilty? What do you think is at the root of your guilt feelings? Are your feelings false guilt or conviction from the Holy Spirit?
- Why is repentance of sin essential? What does repentance mean to you?
- Why are you no longer guilty before God the Father? Find a Scripture verse to support your answer.
- How will you deal with feelings of guilt the next time they come?
- Which Bible truths can help you avoid this trap?

My Thoughts:

_____

_____

_____

_____

_____
_____
_____
_____
_____
_____
_____
_____
_____
_____
_____
_____
_____
_____
_____
_____
_____
_____
_____
_____
_____
_____
_____
_____

DAY 2
COMPARISON GAME

"I'm bigger than you are!" "No, you're not. I'm bigger!" Have you ever heard this kind of argument? You probably have because it is a common occurrence among children. It may be about who is stronger, who's smarter, who's prettier, or who is taller. Children often compare themselves to one another. But it is not only common among children.

Which one of us has not fallen into the trap of comparing ourselves to someone else? We compare our clothes, figure, weight, accomplishments, abilities, company positions, ministries, and even our spouses and children. We all are prone to compare ourselves with others in one way or another.

Why do we do this? Is it a means to make ourselves feel better, or are we looking for evidence to enforce our feelings of unworthiness?

"To compare is a fundamental human impulse, and our social media feeds it. The narrow, distorted slice of reality that is displayed is constructed to make viewers feel deficient and discouraged. Social media is like kerosene poured on the flame of social comparison, dramatically increasing information about people that we are exposed to and forcing our minds to assess"[11]

As believers, we are not OF this world, but we are IN it and continuously exposed to its influence. It is evident that comparing ourselves to others stems from our old nature and is encouraged by our enemy.

This trap is not new. The disciples also fell into it. "Then there arose a reasoning among them, which of them should be the greatest" (Luke 9:46). Even Peter compared his commitment to the Lord to that of the other disciples. "Peter answered and said unto him, Though all men shall be offended because of thee, yet will I never be offended" (Matthew 26:33).

"We compare ourselves to others, get lost in their idealized lives, and forget to enjoy our own," states Emma Seppaelae, science director of the Center for Compassion and Altruism Research and Education at Stanford University.[12]

I once compared myself to a particular family whose lives appeared close to perfect. They had money, their own business, health, prestige, a beautiful home, and successful children. Comparing their lives to mine led to feelings of envy and discontentment, but I only saw the outside.

Years down the road, I was surprised to discover the couple did not have a happy marriage, their business had financial problems, and their children were a long way from perfect. I could almost hear the Lord asking me, "So what exactly have you been envious of?"

It took time for me to realize my view of these people came from what I saw looking on the outside. I could not see the reality on the inside. I had been foolish and carnal minded for envying and overlooking my blessings.

Comparing ourselves to others is a deadly trap of our enemy. It opens the door to pride, jealousy, envy, and discontentment. "For where envying and strife is, there is confusion and every evil work" (James 3:16).

How can we avoid getting caught in this trap? We can start by accepting ourselves as our Designer made us. Each of us is unique on purpose, and our value is in Christ, not in how we line up with someone else.

Our talents and abilities differ, but these do not affect our worth. "For who maketh thee to differ from another? And what hast thou that thou didst not receive? now if thou didst receive it, why dost thou glory, as if thou hadst not received it?" (1 Corinthians 4:7).

Despite what we may think, no one life puzzle is more important or more valuable than another. A godly mother in a secluded part of the world, raising her children to love and obey God, is just as valuable as a famous evangelist who preaches to thousands every week. It is not what we do nor the opinion of those around us that determines our value. It is our obedience and the motive in our hearts that matter. "For the Lord seeth as man seeth; for man looketh on the outward appearance, but the Lord looketh on the heart" (1 Samuel 16:7b). It is about doing what our Designer gives us to do.

Another way to avoid the comparison trap is to develop a thankful heart. Instead of dwelling on what we don't have or cannot do, we can think about all the blessings in our lives. "Bless the Lord, O my soul, and forget not all his benefits" (Psalm 103:2).

According to an article posted in the magazine *Psychology Today*, gratitude has six benefits.[13]

1. It improves physical health.
2. It improves psychological health by reducing the toxic emotions of envy and resentment.
3. It reduces aggression and depression.
4. It improves sleep.
5. It increases mental strength. It helps relieve stress and plays a major role in overcoming trauma.
6. Being thankful for and even during the worst times fosters resilience.

"Giving thanks always for all things unto God and the Father in the name of our Lord Jesus Christ" (Ephesians 5:20).

Exercising discipline in our thinking, accepting our differences, recognizing the value in our uniqueness, and expressing thanksgiving and praise to our Designer will help us avoid the dangerous trap of comparing. It will also raise our level of joy and contentment in life.

Dig Deeper:
- What are you thankful for in your life and about yourself?
- In what situation have you found yourself playing the comparing game? What did you compare?
- How did this affect you and your walk with your Designer?
- Do you like yourself? If not, why not?
- Ask your Designer to show you the root problem behind your struggle with comparing?

My Thoughts:

_____

_____

_____

_____

_____

_____

_____

_____

_____

_____

_____

_____

_____

_____

DAY 3
DISTRACTIONS

The race nears its end, and you can almost feel the adrenalin spike as anticipation in the audience rises. Headed for the finish line, the runners kick in their last boost of energy, and the people jump to their feet, shouting and cheering for their favorite runner. The clock is ticking; time is running out. Everyone braces for the finish when suddenly the crowd gasps. The lead runner goes down. Shock, horror, and unbelief engulf the stadium. Oh, no, what happened? Is the runner injured?

Immediately the onlookers speculate on what could have happened. Did he have a heart attack? Did he trip over something in his lane, or did he get distracted?

Perhaps distraction did cause the runner to fall and consequently to lose the race. Statistics reveal just how deadly distractions can be. According to the National Highway Traffic Safety Association, over the last ten years, 11,100 injuries have occurred, and 5,376 people have died while walking. How has walking become so dangerous? Distractions related to cell phones were frequently the cause.

We know many auto accidents occur every year from various causes. But did you know that in 2018, according to a report from the National Highway Traffic Safety Administration (NHTSA), 2,841 people died as a result of distracted drivers?

Anything that distracts our attention from what we are doing can be hazardous. This is true whether we are walking, driving, running a piece of machinery, raising our children, building a godly marriage, or in our daily walk with our Designer.

Our world explodes with noise and busyness. Our cell phones and the internet bombard us with information. We receive a steady stream of news, sound bites, updates, pictures, video clips, recipes, prayer requests, and general information from family, friends, and acquaintances.

None of these things in themselves is wrong, and they can be a blessing. But they can also be destructive when they rob our time, distract our thoughts, and hinder us from following our Designer. The greater our desire to walk close to Him, the harder our enemy works to distract and hinder us.

Have you noticed how things interrupt and distract our prayer time and Bible study? We begin reading our Bible and the phone rings, we get a message on our cell phone, someone knocks on the door, or the baby wakes up. Are these occurrences merely coincidences, or is our enemy behind them?

When we finally get to our devotions and begin reading the Bible, we find our minds drifting to what we will cook for lunch or what we need to do later. Our thoughts wander. Our eyes see the words, but our concentration is somewhere else. We might finish our planned reading, but the verses will have little effect on our lives because of distractions.

Scripture admonishes us to "lay aside every weight, and the sin which doth so easily beset us, and let us run with patience the race that is set before us, looking unto Jesus the author and finisher of our faith" (Hebrews 12:1-2a). Let us keep the right focus and not allow the allurements or pleasures of this world to distract us.

Have you ever been distracted because you were looking at the life of someone else? Jesus had just instructed Peter to follow Him when Peter turns, looks at John, and asks, "Lord, and what shall this man do?" Jesus quickly put a stop to Peter's speculation and told him it was none of his business. His job was to tend to his own life.

Preparing a special meal distracted Martha. "And Martha was cumbered about much serving, and came to him, and said, Lord, doest thou not care that my sister hath left me to serve alone? Bid her therefore that she help me" (Luke 10:40). Jesus told Martha she was missing the important part. The part that really mattered was spending time with Jesus.

We can also become preoccupied with problems in our lives or in the lives of those we love. Our focus becomes fixed on what WE think is important. When this happens, human logic overrides faith and opens the door to temptations and wrong priorities. It can take us down a path of defeat and unfruitfulness. "And the cares of this world, and the deceitfulness of things entering in, choke the word, and it becometh unfruitful" (Mark 4:19). Worry and the deceitful ways of the world around us can keep us from being spiritually fruitful.

Since distractions are so prevalent, how can we avoid or limit them? The first step is self-discipline. A lady in our church calls this the ugly D word because it does not come easy. It requires us to take responsibility for our behavior and to be intentional with our thinking.

The next step in guarding against distractions is to have quality time with our Designer before we become involved in the activities of the day. Praying and asking our Designer to lead us before we start surfing the internet, watching tube clips or any other social media activity will help us make wise decisions. Checking Facebook, responding to friends, and checking in with groups we are connected to can also eat hours of our time and cause us to become distracted and draw our thoughts away from our Designer.

"For though we walk in the flesh, we do not war after the flesh: For the weapons of our warfare are not carnal, but mighty through God to the pulling down of strongholds; casting down imaginations, and every high thing that exalteth itself against the knowledge of God, and bringing into captivity every thought to the obedience of Christ" (2 Corinthians 10:3-5).

Exercising discipline in our thought life is essential since thoughts dictate our actions. It is easy to let our thoughts wander or become wrapped up in our emotions and desires. Disciplining our thoughts means staying alert to what we think and exercising our will to make the right choices. God's Word gives us examples and guidelines to help us.

Keeping his focus on the invisible, spiritual goal enabled Moses to carry out the immense task of leading the children of Israel out of Egypt to the Promised Land. "By faith he forsook Egypt, not fearing the wrath of the king: for he endured, as seeing him who is invisible" (Hebrews 11:27).

A spiritual focus enabled Paul to handle the persecution, mistreatment, pain, imprisonment, misunderstandings, and the struggles of the ministry he encountered. "But this one thing I do, forgetting those things which are behind, and reaching forth unto those things which are before, I press toward the mark for the prize of the high calling of God in Christ Jesus" (Philippians 4:12-13).

When distractions come, remember: we have a choice. We can yield and follow where they may lead us or we can exert self-discipline and rely on our Designer to help us resist them.

"There hath no temptation taken you but such as is common to man: but God is faithful, who will not suffer you to be tempted above that ye are able; but will with the temptation also make a way to escape, that ye may be able to bear it" (1 Corinthians 10:13).

Dig Deeper:

- What do you think the weights Hebrews 12:1 refers to are? How can they hinder in living for our Designer?
- What distracts you from putting your Designer first in your life, in your priorities. How can you avoid these things?
- When Jesus was on the earth, on what did He focus? Read John 5:19, 6:38, 14:31; Matthew 26:39
- Read Psalm 25:15. How can you apply this verse to your life?

My Thoughts:

_____

_____

_____

_____

_____

_____

_____

_____

_____

_____

_____

_____

_____

_____

_____

_____

_____

DAY 4
SEARCH FOR SELF-WORTH

I want to make a difference. I want the world to be better because I lived. These were my thoughts as a young adult. As I grew older, I recognized I was not the only one with this desire. People naturally want to feel valuable; to believe their lives matter.

The desire for our lives to have value is not the problem but rather how and where we seek to fulfill it. Instead of looking to the one who designed us, we often look to people and the things of this world.

We turn to prosperity, popularity, position, or affirmation through our jobs, churches, clubs, hobbies, good works, or Christian service. We seek to find something or someone to make us feel important, to give our lives purpose.

Our enemy, Satan, is well aware of our need. He dangles worldly significance in front of us, coaxing us farther and farther away from the source of our real value. He may even give us some recognition as an appetizer, but he cannot satisfy the deep hunger within us.

Some secular psychologists focus on self-worth as merely a need to feel good about ourselves. As a means to accomplish this, our society has brain-washed us into believing a formula for determining our self-worth: ABILITY TO PERFORM + OPINIONS OF OTHERS = SELF-WORTH. This formula presents a serious dilemma.

The level of our performance on the job, at home as a spouse and parent, in clubs and sports, or in various ministries at church can radically change. We can have an accident, become ill, have a baby, hit a financial crisis, go through a divorce, or merely grow older. Any of these changes, as well as countless other factors, can influence our level of productivity. When our performance level goes down, according to the society's judgment, our value is decreased.

What about the opinions of others—the judgment of our peers, family, and co-workers? It is shocking to me to see how quickly not only the standards of society have changed, but also the views, attitudes, and focus of many Christian circles. What happens to my personal convictions if I am concerned with having the approval of others?

There was a time when I used society's formula. When I began having health issues in 1978, they limited my ability to accomplish my work. Since I felt my value was affected by what I accomplished or did not accomplish, I felt discouraged. This situation accelerated until my husband decided for us to leave the mission field. Now I felt like a failure.

When depression moved in, I swore my husband to secrecy because I was afraid of my peers' disapproval. I knew that many fellow Christians believed depression was the result of some hidden sin, and I did not want their judgment or criticism. It was apparent to me that, according to the world's formula for self-worth, I had little value.

This formula will lead us to take control of putting our life puzzle together away from our Designer. It will send us down a path of self-centeredness infested with fear, frustration, rejection, insecurity, and instability.

The good news is we can avoid this trap and find valid significance and self-worth. The solution is accepting our Designer's equation: GOD'S TRUTH ABOUT US = OUR SELF-WORTH. (And His truth never changes!)

What is God's truth about us and our value?

1. Our Designer created each of us uniquely ON purpose WITH a purpose.
2. We are redeemed children of God.
3. We are in Christ, and He is in us.
4. We are a holy temple of the indwelling Holy Spirit who will empower us to accomplish the will of our Designer.

Did you notice none of the four points is affected by age, wealth, education, health, physical ability, social standing, or any other aspect under our control? This truth is fantastic because it means our value and significance are secure and permanent in Christ. "Significance is not a search; it is a gift."[14]

We can choose to listen to the philosophy of society under the influence of Satan, the father of lies, or we can listen to our Designer who is the essence of truth and cannot lie.

Dig Deeper:
- What makes you feel important, and why?
- What effect has the world's view of self-worth had on you?
- Do your failures affect your value? If so, how?
- What changes would result if you accepted God's formula for determining your self-worth?

Write out the four points listed above in your own words. Re-read them two or three times a week, claim them for yourself, and thank your Designer for the value He has given you.

My Thoughts:

_____

_____

_____

DAY 5
HANGING ONTO THE PAST

Hanging onto the past will keep us from taking hold of the future. Our enemy likes to trigger stored memories of painful, traumatic experiences, toxic relationships, shameful failures, or broken trusts. Remembering these toxic events will block us from moving into the present and accepting what our Designer has for us to do.

What if Moses had not been able to let go of the murder he committed? Could Paul have preached God's truth if he could not have turned loose of the way he previously persecuted believers? What about Joseph? What would have happened if he had not forgiven his brothers?

Not letting go of the past leads to self-condemnation, self-pity, anger, and bitterness, which destroys our joy and peace. Since we cannot undo or rewind the past, we need to let it go and move forward, but how?

Moving forward does not mean we no longer remember the traumatic experience from the past, but it does mean we do not allow it to control the present. The key is forgiveness.

The idea of forgiving someone for a cruel or evil act they have committed against us may appear impossible, and it is in our own strength. But if it was impossible, then our Designer would have never commanded us to forgive. "Forbearing one another, and forgiving one another, if any man have a quarrel against any: even as Christ forgave you, so also do ye" (Colossians 3:13).

Secular medical books classify unforgiveness as a disease. Dr. Steven Stanford, chief of surgery at the Cancer Treatment Center of America, says refusing to forgive makes people sick and keeps them that way.[15]

108 | UNPUZZLING YOUR *Life*

An article from the Johns Hopkins medical magazine says unforgiveness turns to chronic anger. "Chronic anger puts you into a fight-or-flight mode, which results in numerous changes in heart rate, blood pressure, and immune response. These changes, then, increase the risk of depression, heart disease, and diabetes, among other conditions. Forgiveness, however, calms stress levels leading to improved health."[16] No wonder our Designer has commanded us to forgive.

The truth is sometimes it is not that we can't forgive but that we don't want to. When the experience is traumatic and painful, our wounded heart balks at forgiving. We want justice, and somehow, we feel by forgiving, it will not happen. We are under the misconception that our forgiveness means the person goes free. Judgment over a sin is always in our Designer's hands. By not forgiving, though, we continue to let the guilty person affect our lives in the present.

Forgiveness does not depend on the worthiness of the offender, the extent of the offense, or the acknowledgment of the wrong. It does not dictate our interaction with the offender in the future. It does mean we will accept living with the consequences of what was done.

To forgive is first and foremost an act of obedience to our Designer. We need to forgive because it is His will and we are His children. He said we are to forgive as He has forgiven us. "And be ye kind one to another, tenderhearted, forgiving one another, even as God for Christ's sake hath forgiven you" (Ephesians 4:32).

Since we are imperfect, it is impossible for us to grasp the depth of our sinfulness before a holy, perfect God. It was so extreme that only the pure sacrifice of God's holy Son could pay the debt it created.

As believers, we are in Christ, and He is in us. The command to forgive is actually a command to yield to the Holy Spirit and let the love of our Designer flow through us.

A few years ago, I taught at a lady's retreat in Siberia. After one of the sessions a lady came to me with tears rolling down her face, and through a translator she told me her story. Her only son was murdered, and she knew who the killer was. She did not inform the police because she said the murderer had two young children, and if he went to prison, the children would have to go to a state-run orphanage. She said, "I could not do that to those children."

Her story moved my heart, but this was not the reason for her tears. She was crying because it took her so long to forgive the killer. When I asked her how long it had been, she answered, "Two months."

To forgive the man who killed your only son in just two months didn't seem long to me. On the contrary, it sounded more like a miracle. Her decision to forgive came after she accepted Christ as her Savior.

What about our sins that haunt us? How can we leave them behind? The first step is to face the facts. Admit what we have done. Don't justify it or excuse it—face it.

The next step is accepting our Designer's forgiveness. All our sins were laid on Him when He was on the cross, including those that haunt us. "But he was wounded for our transgressions, he was bruised for our iniquities: the chastisement of our peace was upon him; and with his stripes we are healed. All we like sheep have gone astray: we have turned everyone to his own way; and the Lord hath laid on him the iniquity of us all" (Isaiah 53:5-6).

He took our punishment. Justice was served. It is finished. Now we need to accept our Designer's forgiveness and be set free.

"If the Son therefore shall make you free, ye shall be free indeed" (John 8:36).

Whenever the enemy reminds you of your sin, stop and claim the truth of God's Word: Your sins are all under the blood. "I, even I, am he that blotteth out thy transgressions for mine own sake, and will not remember thy sins" (Isaiah 43:25). "If we confess our sins, he is faithful and just to forgive us our sins, and to cleanse us from all unrighteousness" (1 John 1:9). If my Designer does not think about my sin, then I don't need to either.

Forgiveness and claiming the truth of God's Word instead of turning to our emotions and human reasoning will enable us to let go of the past. In Aramaic, the word for forgiveness is *shbag* and means "to untie." By God's grace, we can untie the past from our present and experience relief, peace, and freedom. It is our choice.

Dig Deeper:
- What are you hanging onto from the past?
- Are you willing to forgive the one who has hurt you? If not, what is hindering you?
- Read John 8:31-32 and 2 Corinthians 3:17. How do these verses relate to overcoming this trap of unforgiveness?
- According to Mark 11:25, what other areas of your life can unforgiveness affect?
- Have you accepted God's forgiveness for yourself?

My Thoughts:

_____

_____

_____

_____

_____

Chapter Five
THE DARK PIECES

No puzzle can be complete with only light-colored pieces. The dark ones are also needed to give depth and perspective. In the same way, our life puzzle requires dark pieces.

These pieces are the unwanted, undesirable, or painful experiences we encounter. When the purpose and duration of such times are unknown, they are especially difficult and can cause us to question as Gideon did. "Oh, my Lord, if the Lord be with us, why then is all this befallen us?" (Judges 6:13).

If we only rely on our human understanding and perception, our emotions can easily spin off into resistance, anger, bitterness, depression, and despair. For this reason, depending on our Designer's Word is vital for us. It will change our perspective and calm our emotions. "For I know the thoughts that I think toward you, saith the Lord, thoughts of peace and not of evil, to give you an expected end" (Jeremiah 29:11).

I am thankful that none of the circumstances or our emotions can hinder our Designer's faithfulness or annul His promises. "Let us hold fast the confession of our hope without wavering, for He who promised is faithful" (Hebrews 10:23).

Although the dark pieces may be difficult to understand, they are essential tools of our Designer's love. In this chapter we want to take a closer look at how this works.

DAY 1
SPIRITUAL WAR

Have you ever been behind enemy lines? Imagine the tension as you are always on alert, anticipating an impending attack but not knowing precisely from which direction it will come. While this scenario isn't on the top of our bucket lists, when we become children of God, this becomes our reality.

We are soldiers given a divine mission and confronted with powerful, spiritual enemies. "For we wrestle not against flesh and blood, but against principalities, against powers, against the rulers of the darkness of this world, against spiritual wickedness in high places" (Ephesians 6:12).

We talked about how Satan can attack our thinking in chapter 4, but that is not the only area he attacks. The story of Job reveals other ways the enemy can interfere and disrupt our lives.

The Designer allowed Satan to take Job's wealth, children, prestige, respect, and health. The enemy was confident that all this loss would cause Job to curse his Designer and turn from Him. The enemy's plan failed. Job held on to his shield of faith and, in the middle of his suffering, said, "Though he slay me, yet will I trust in him" (Job 13:15).

Not only did Job remain faithful, but his Designer used the ordeal to bring about good and blessings in his life. Job's experience humbled his heart and brought him new spiritual insight and awareness of his Designer. "I have heard of thee by the hearing of the ear: but now mine eye seeth thee" (Job 42:5-6).

This new and intimate reality with his Designer was not all Job received. The material blessings were abundant. He received double the amount of his previous wealth, and his Designer miraculously restored his health and strength. Job regained his standing and respect in the community, and, perhaps the most precious of all, he was given ten more beautiful children. Not only did Job live to father ten more children, but he also experienced his great-great-grandchildren.

Satan's attacks on us do not go unnoticed by our Designer and can, in fact, only come with His permission. Their purpose is to bring about spiritual change and blessing.

Mrs. Pearl Gibbs was a young wife and mother when polio invaded her body. Her illness shocked and saddened her family. Her young son, David, had an incredibly hard time accepting it. His mom loved the Lord and was a faithful, active member of her church. Why would God allow this to happen?

After two years of care in hospitals and rehabilitation facilities, Mrs. Gibbs returned home. Convinced her Designer still had work for her to do, she refused to be discouraged by the paralysis claiming most of her body.

One evening, a young pastor visited the Gibbs home and asked Mrs. Gibbs if she thought she could teach a Sunday school class. She immediately replied that she would do her best, and she did. Her Designer blessed it, and the number of children in

Sunday school grew so much that they needed a bus to transport them. But the church did not have a bus, nor did they have money to buy one. What could they do?

Mrs. Gibbs decided she would ask the bus company to give them one. She asked her son David to drive her there. Reluctantly, David agreed. It was a cold winter day, and packed snow and ice covered the bus company's parking lot. David parked the car and went around to help his Mom out, protesting that no company would just GIVE the church a bus.

Suddenly, a piercing scream of agony cut through the cold winter morning. While moving his paralyzed mother from the car to her wheelchair, David lost his grip and dropped her onto the frozen, snow-covered parking lot.

For thirty minutes waves of pain surged through the body of Mrs. Gibbs. At last, the pain lessened and she let her son know she was ready to be moved. David managed to lift his mother from the frozen ground and set her in her wheelchair.

"Mom, God is not in this or He would not have let me drop you. Please, let's just go home."

Mrs. Gibbs remained undaunted in her purpose. She had come to get a bus to pick up children for Sunday school at her church.

"Davey, now clean up my face," she said. "I don't want them to see I have been crying. We are going to get our bus."

This decision made no sense to David, but he obeyed his mother and reluctantly pushed her wheelchair into the building.

Mrs. Gibbs was finally able to speak with the bus company's owner, and he immediately recognized her as the woman he had observed from his window. "Lady, you parked right under my office window. I saw you fall. I heard your cries. I never saw a bus mean so much to anyone before, but I can't just give you a bus."

"If you don't give me a bus, one day when you stand before the Lord, He is going to be awfully upset with you," Mrs. Gibbs warned.

"But if I do give you a bus, who will drive it?"

Puzzled for a moment, Mrs. Gibbs replied, "You're right. I need a bus AND a driver."

"All right," the bus owner conceded. "I will give you one bus and one driver for one week."

Their conversation continued, and the bus owner consented to supply two buses with two drivers for two weeks. Within a year, the bus company provided thirty-five buses and drivers and continued to do so for twenty-two years.

More precious than the buses were the children who rode on them and came to know Christ as their Savior. The bus company owner, his vice president, and their families, and many of the bus drivers became God's children.

Satan may have thought his attack would stop Mrs. Gibbs from serving her Designer and bring bitterness to her family's hearts. But just the opposite took place. Mrs. Gibbs had a powerful testimony and remained active for her Designer for seventy-six years. David grew and became the founder and president of the Christian Law Association.

The war is real, and attacks will come, but keep in mind that our Lord knows what is happening and has given us all we need to stand firm against our enemies. "Wherefore take unto you the whole armour of God, that ye may be able to withstand in the evil day, and having done all to stand" (Ephesians 6:13).

Dig Deeper:

- Why do you think the Designer allowed Satan to attack Job? (Job 1:6-12) Write out your answer.

- Is there a time in your life when you were under physical attack? What did you learn from it, or what blessings resulted?
- What can we do to stay alert to our enemy and to prepare for the battle? Make a list of verses that can help you.

How can we encourage others when they are going through heavy trials?

My Thoughts:

_____

_____

_____

_____

_____

_____

_____

_____

_____

_____

_____

_____

_____

_____

_____

_____

_____

_____

_____

_____

_____

DAY 2
CRUSHING AND REFINING

In 1848, the California gold rush was sparked by the discovery of gold nuggets in the Sacramento Valley. As news spread, people flocked to California in search of this precious metal and with dreams of finding riches. Two billion dollars' worth of gold was extracted from the area in just a few years. Finding the gold through panning in the streams or in chipping it out of a mountain was just the beginning. It still needed to be refined.

Can you picture an old craftsman sitting by a crackling fire with a pair of tongs in his weathered hand, carefully holding a crucible full of nuggets? Although he can feel the intense heat of the fire, he keeps the crucible in the hottest part of the flame and watches as the metal begins to bubble and melt. It is a dangerous job as the temperature of the fire can rise to more than 1000 degrees Celsius.

As the metal heats, the impurities rise to the surface. The craftsman then carefully skims them off the top and returns the crucible to the fire. Time and time again, he skims impurities off until the gold is pure...until the old craftsman can see his reflection in the gold. The crucible never leaves the craftsman's hand, and he keeps a careful watch on the fire lest excessive heat should mar the precious metal. The fire is not meant to consume but to purify.

This is a familiar analogy and one that can help us understand another purpose for the dark pieces in our life. Just as the gold ore had to be crushed and then purified so must we be broken and refined.

Our Designer used family, slavery, and jail to break and refine Joseph. Peter had to go through denying Christ to realize his insufficiency. The process required forty years on the backside of a desert for Moses.

According to Webster's dictionary, the word *refine* means "to free from impurities or to make pure," and nothing reveals and brings the impurities of our old nature to the surface more than tribulation and affliction. The dark pieces are our Designer's refining fire. "That the trial of your faith being much more precious than of gold that perisheth, though it be tried with fire, might be found unto praise and honor and glory at the appearing of Jesus Christ" (1 Peter 1:7).

In my case, health issues and depression were the fire my Designer chose. I did not realize the extent of my self-righteousness and rebellion until my Designer began working. The heat increased and my situation grew consistently worse until it felt as if my Designer laid my heart wide open and said, "Now take a good look inside."

I was shocked and ashamed when I saw the depth of my pride and my sinful, ungodly desires as these impurities rose to the top. As my Designer began skimming these out of my heart, it felt as though He were doing surgery without anesthesia.

Oswald Chambers said, "What we need is God's surgical procedure—His use of external circumstances to bring about internal purification."[17]

Remembering that old craftsman and his crucible of gold can remind us that dark pieces may well be our Designer's refining fire to bring about His reflection in our lives.

"My brethren, count it all joy when ye fall into divers temptations: knowing this, that the trying of your faith worketh patience. But let patience have its perfect work, that ye may be perfect and entire, wanting nothing" (James 1:2-4).

Dig Deeper:

- Read James 1:3-4. How can you apply these verses to the dark pieces in your life?
- Read James 1:12. What blessings come from trials?
- How do you feel when your Designer puts you in His refining fire?
- What blessings have you received through the refining experiences in your life?

My Thoughts:

_____
_____
_____
_____
_____
_____
_____
_____
_____
_____
_____
_____
_____
_____
_____
_____
_____
_____
_____
_____

DAY 3
LOVE PROMPTED DISCIPLINE

"Do you want a spanking?" Did you ever hear your mom or dad say this to you when you were young? When I heard these words, I knew it was not a question but a warning. My parents took a strong position on obedience and did not hesitate to exercise discipline when it was needed. Needless to say, I did not enjoy those times.

Most of us do not look forward to being disciplined, but it is necessary and extremely important. When loving parents see their children doing something that will harm them or are headed in a direction that will result in grief and pain, they will do whatever they can to stop them. This often involves some form of discipline and is for the children's benefit.

Discipline in our lives, as children of our Designer, is similar. When we choose to disobey His commands and get involved in ungodly ways, our Designer cannot ignore it. He loves us too much to let us continue in a direction that will not only bring hurt and destruction but will move us from the place of blessing.

Correction will not fall immediately. The Holy Spirit will bring conviction to our hearts clearly showing us our sin. The pastor may preach a sermon that just happens to be about the very sin we are committing. A godly friend may speak a warning or rebuke under the direction of the Holy Spirit. Our Designer will try to get our attention and turn our hearts to repentance. If we resist, though, He will use discipline, and we can be sure it will always fit the crime.

We have a choice on how we will respond. We can get upset or become disheartened. These are likely reactions if we forget why we are being disciplined. "My children, despise not thou the chastening of the Lord, nor faint when thou art rebuked of him: for whom the Lord loveth he chasteneth, and scourgeth every son whom he receiveth" (Hebrews 12:5-6).

King David was a child of our Designer and, according to Scripture, a man after God's own heart. But David sinned greatly when he took Bathsheba, another man's wife, and then had her husband killed. The discipline that followed was hard—the death of his newborn son.

How did David react to this? Did he get angry at his Designer and claim it was unfair? Did he sink into depression and give up his position as king? No, David did not react in either of these ways.

David knew his Designer loved him and relied on that fact. "Have mercy upon me, O God, according to thy lovingkindness: according unto the multitude of thy tender mercies blot out my transgressions" (Psalm 51:1).

He accepted responsibility for his sinful actions and confessed his sin. "Wash me thoroughly from mine iniquity, and cleanse me from my sin. For I acknowledge my transgressions: my sin is ever before me" (Psalm 51:2-3). The Designer's discipline did the work it was meant to do.

David was confronted with his sin, accepted responsibility, repented, and received the forgiveness of his Designer. The broken fellowship was restored. Toward the end of his life David recognized the benefit of the discipline he received. "Before I was afflicted I went astray: but now have I kept thy word. It is good for me that I have been afflicted; that I might learn thy statutes" (Psalm 119:67, 71).

The discipline may be painful for a while, but when we yield as David did, in the long run it will bring great benefit. "Now no chastening for the present seemeth to be joyous, but grievous: nevertheless afterward it yieldeth the peaceable fruit of righteousness unto them which are exercised thereby" (Hebrews 12:11). It will bring about repentance, restored fellowship, and spiritual growth.

I can testify to the benefits of divine discipline. The spiritual lessons I learned through the dark pieces my Designer used in my life radically changed my relationship with Him. It went from a relationship based on fear to one based on love. This transformation was worth all the pain involved.

C. H. Spurgeon, a well-known and powerful preacher of the twentieth century, said, "I bear my willing witness that I owe more to the fire, and the hammer, and the file, than to anything else in my Lord's workshop. I sometimes question whether I have ever learned anything except through the rod. When my school room is darkened, I see the most."[18]

"Blessed is the man whom thou chastenest, O Lord, and teachest him out of thy law" (Psalm 94:12).

Dig Deeper:

- How has your Designer used discipline in your life?
- Can you think of something you learned in the dark times? How did it benefit you in your life? Explain.
- Read Proverbs 3:11. What do you think this verse means?
- Can you think of someone else in the Bible who learned from God's discipline?

My Thoughts:

_____

_____

_____

_____

_____

DAY 4
HIDDEN TREASURES

For centuries, the idea of finding a hidden treasure has intrigued men and driven them to invest vast amounts of money, effort, and time in the search. Some have spent their whole lives hoping to find hidden wealth. Would it surprise you to know that you and I have a hidden treasure more valuable than anything on earth?

Paul tells us what this treasure is. "For God, who commanded the light to shine out of darkness, hath shined in our hearts, to give the light of the knowledge of the glory of God in the face of Jesus Christ. But we have this treasure in earthen vessels, that the excellency of the power may be of God, and not of us" (2 Corinthians 4:6-7).

Our treasure is Christ and His power working in and through us. Of course, our Designer is not hidden from us, but we may not have discovered the treasure of His power. The dark pieces which push us beyond our strength, endurance, and abilities open up the opportunity for us to discover this treasure.

"We are troubled on every side, yet not distressed; we are perplexed, but not in despair; persecuted, but not forsaken; cast down, but not destroyed; always bearing about in the body the dying of the Lord Jesus, that the life also of Jesus might be made manifest in our body" (2 Corinthians 4:8-10).

Any time we can do what we could never do in ourselves, we reveal our Designer's power. It may be having hope when conditions look hopeless or exhibiting peace when sickness hits our family and finances run low. It may be loving the unlovable or accepting our Designer's will when it means separation and loss.

In 2019, a couple in our church were expecting their third child. Early in the pregnancy doctors detected a major problem.

The baby's heart and head were not forming right, and if they did not improve, the baby would have no chance for life.

As time went by, the baby's heart grew stronger, but her little head still was not forming as it should. We were all praying, and the parents hoped the condition of their baby would improve. Each month, the doctor's report was mixed: some areas improved, but one big issue remained. Although the parents were burdened for their unborn child, they continued to trust their Designer and stayed faithful in church.

The time of delivery drew near. Parts of the baby's head and skull were not formed. The mother, with a heavy heart, accepted the fact that her little one would not live. She did, however, make one request of her Designer: *let me hold her just a little before You take her to heaven.*

The time came, and the baby was delivered. A nurse wrapped little Nora in a cozy, warm blanket, put a stocking cap on her head to hide the malformation, and handed her to her mother. Nora lived one hour and fifteen minutes. She opened her eyes and let out a weak, soft cry as her mother held her close.

The father and two siblings were also there, and they were able to take a family photo. Her mother received her wish. The strength and faith of this family demonstrated the reality of their Designer's power. Their lives revealed the divine treasure.

The baby's funeral revealed yet another treasure: a song in the night. Baby Nora's mother wrote and sang a song of dedication to her daughter and thankfulness to her Designer. The ability to sing praises to our Designer when our hearts are broken and the dark pieces feel so heavy is a rare and precious treasure. I think we can only find it when we are confident of His love and assured His purpose is for good.

In the sixteenth chapter of the book of Acts, we can read how Paul and Silas healed a young woman of demon possession. As a result, the disciples did not receive gratitude but were beaten, put in stocks, and thrown into prison. According to ancient historians, the prison where they were could have been called the House of Darkness. The inner cell where these men were taken was known for its darkness, cold, and stench.

Imagine Paul and Silas, their backs bleeding from open wounds, being thrown into this inner cell and their feet fastened in rough, wooden stocks. Often these wooden stocks made it impossible for the prisoners to sit or stand, so they had to lie on the cold, filthy, stone floor. I wonder how we would react in this situation? Paul and Silas prayed and sang praises to God! (Acts 16:22-25).

How was this possible? They discovered the treasure of songs in the night. "Behold, God is my salvation; I will trust, and not be afraid: for the Lord JEHOVAH is my strength and my song; he also is become my salvation" (Isaiah 12:2).

What happened as a result of the divine power working in and through those men? Their Designer worked miracles, and their faith was blessed.

Remember the mother of Nora? Her Designer worked a miracle in her life too. Not only was she an inspiration to many, but she conceived again and now has a healthy little girl. The *dark* pieces are the perfect place to reveal the life of our Designer in our mortal flesh (2 Corinthians 4:11).

Dig Deeper:
- In what situations have you experienced your Designer's power working in your life? How did it manifest itself?
- Read Psalm 42:5-8. How can you apply these verses to your life?

- Explain in your own words how we can *sing* in the dark times. Make a list of the Bible verses that can encourage your heart.
- Read Habakkuk 3:17-19. What do these verses teach us about the relationship of circumstances and being able to sing praises to our Designer?
- How does Matthew 7:24-27 relate to 2 Corinthians 4:6-7?

My Thoughts:

_____
_____
_____
_____
_____
_____
_____
_____
_____
_____
_____
_____
_____
_____
_____
_____
_____
_____
_____

DAY 5
FINDING THE SECRET PLACE

"He that dwelleth in the secret place of the most High shall abide under the shadow of the Almighty" (Psalm 91:1).

The thought of abiding in a secret place close to our Designer and sheltered from the hate, violence, and wickedness of this world sounds wonderful. But how do we get there when we are struggling in the dark times?

Our hearts are hurting, and we desperately need comfort and compassion. We go to our mate or best friend hoping they can meet our need. They try to understand and offer their advice, maybe give us a hug; but somehow what they offer does not stop the hurt. They leave, we are alone, and the pain continues.

We get word from the doctor that the test reveals stage four cancer. Suddenly, all the material things that were important yesterday lose their value. Now we desperately long for a thread of hope and the strength to carry us through what is ahead. We quickly realize medicine is limited, and it cannot provide what we need most.

Expectations and demands from family, work, friends, and even church are overwhelming, and our minds are on overload. So much to do and too little time and energy. We realize we lack wisdom and discernment. Where can we get what we need? Is there no place of peace, no place of rest?

Dark pieces, regardless of their form, show us our need and insufficiency. They reveal the inability of people and the world to meet our deepest needs and satisfy the hunger in our souls. The dark times come to drive us to the secret place.

To dwell with someone is the same as abiding and means we live together; we spend time together. We want to be close to the person we are with and get to know them better. To dwell in the secret place of the Almighty means to make a conscious, deliberate decision to leave the things of this world behind and to focus all our attention exclusively on our Designer.

If we want to abide in this intimate place, then we will seek to live a holy life. We will put our ungodly habits and practices aside and make no provision for indulging our fleshly desires. When we know our weakness in a certain area, then we will avoid getting into a situation to tempt ourselves. What we watch, listen to, and spend our time on will now be determined by what draws us closer to our Designer and encourages our walk with Him.

The second part of the verse says that if we dwell in the secret place we will abide under the shadow of the Almighty. Think about that for a minute. How close do we need to be to someone to stay in their shadow? Abiding under His shadow indicates a constant, consistent closeness. It means when He moves, we move; where He goes, we go. We cease leading and commence following. "My sheep hear my voice…and they follow me" (John 10:27).

Our Designer desires each of us to dwell with Him in the secret place, and He lovingly orchestrates the pieces of our lives to draw us there. "Come to me…and I will give you rest." (Matthew 11:28).

Dig Deeper:

- What does abide in the secret place of the Almighty mean to you?
- What steps do you need to take in your life to abide under His shadow?
- What do you think might hinder you from getting in this place?

- Make a list of other verses in the Bible that talk about our abiding in Christ.

My Thoughts:

_____

_____

_____

_____

_____

_____

_____

_____

_____

_____

_____

_____

_____

_____

_____

_____

_____

_____

_____

_____

_____

_____

_____

_____

Chapter Six
THE IMPORTANCE OF FAITH

Everyone lives by faith. We drive through a green light at an intersection in faith that the light on the other side is red and the traffic from that direction will stop. We believe the earth will continue to rotate on its axis and revolve around the sun at a constant speed. We set our clocks and calendars in this faith. The laws governing our universe are some of the most trustworthy objects of faith we have.

We visit the doctor having faith that what he directs us to do will improve our health. Every religion directs faith to something or someone. But the validity of faith depends on its object. Is the person and/or object reliable?

The only perfect, unchanging object of faith is not a man or anything made by man. It is the Creator of all things, our Designer, Jesus Christ. His immutability lays the ground for our faith in

Him. "God is not man, that he should lie; neither the son of man, that he should repent: hath he said, and shall he not do it? Or hath he spoken, and shall he not make it good?" (Numbers 23:19).

Genuine, biblical faith is indispensable in the life of a believer. It is what equips us to follow our Designer willingly as He puts our life puzzle together. In this week's study we will consider some essential aspects of faith.

DAY 1
WHAT IS GENUINE FAITH?

Genuine, or biblical, faith is more than intellectual consent to a truth or a promise of our Designer. This kind of faith is more than just believing He exists. The demons know very well that their Designer exists, but they do not trust Him or rely on Him. On the contrary, they deliberately rebel against His authority.

In Scripture the words *believe* and *faith* are sometimes used interchangeably. To help give some clarity to the rest of this chapter, we need to consider two Greek words: *pisteuo*, which means "to have faith: to put trust in"; and *pistis*, which means "persuasion or conviction something is true." These two words, although quite similar, are different.

John 3:16 tells us that whoever believes in Christ will be saved forever. "Whosoever believeth in him should not perish but have everlasting life." In this verse, *pisteuo* is used and is the same word used in Romans 10:9: "That if thou shalt confess with thy mouth the Lord Jesus and shalt believe in thine heart that God hath raised him from the dead, thou shalt be saved."

When we hear the gospel, that Jesus loves us and shed His blood for our sins, the Holy Spirit does a work in our hearts. He draws us to recognize our need for the Savior. If we want this price-less gift of forgiveness and eternal life, we must make a deliberate, conscious decision to believe and put our trust in our Designer. By this act of believing, we become His child. This is *pisteuo* faith.

Hebrews 11:1 speaks about a faith that can claim the reality of something not yet seen. The word used here is *pistis.* This word indicates growth from the faith exercised in John 3:16. This faith is persuaded, absolutely convinced that our Designer will do what He promised. A story in the Old Testament illustrates this kind of faith.

A mighty coalition of fighting men was preparing to go against the Israelites. As they surrounded Jerusalem, Jehoshaphat, the leader of the Israelites at the time, was filled with fear. He knew he did not have the men or the means to fight the multitude surrounding the city. He came before God confessing their dependence and need of help. The Lord said, "Be not afraid nor dismayed by reason of this great multitude; for the battle is not yours, but God's" (2 Chronicles 20:15).

Believing God would fight for them went against all human reason, but they made a choice and exercised faith. They appointed singers to go before the army, and they sang songs of praise and victory as they marched into battle. Although they had not yet won the victory, they were sure, based on what God had said, that they would. Their faith reaped the reward. God kept His word, and they won the battle.

Some might argue, yes, but that was then, and times are different now. Times and our needs may be different, but our Designer is not. "Jesus Christ the same yesterday, and today, and forever" (Hebrews 13:8). Our Designer will keep His promises to us. "Let us hold fast the profession of our faith without wavering; (for he is faithful that promised)" (Hebrews 10:23).

When my mother moved into an assisted living facility, I had the job of clearing her large home and then selling it. This challenge was a new experience for me. I had never owned a house, let alone sold one. As if this challenge was not enough, I only had six weeks to get it done.

All I could do was lay it out before the Lord and trust Him to help me. "Lord, You know this is not a wish or a luxury, but a true need. My mother cannot afford to stay where she is without selling her house. You also know how long I have to get this done. So, because You have promised to meet our needs, I will thank You in advance for helping us and for sending us a buyer."

As soon as I arrived, the Lord provided an excellent realtor my mother liked, which was remarkable. She and my mother hit it off right away, and they put the house on the market. I began sorting and cleaning.

We gave things to family and friends. We loaded clothes and some of the smaller things into the car and dropped them off at Good Will and the Veterans Association. Within five weeks we were ready for an estate sale, and the Lord had given us a buyer for the house. It was the first family that looked at the house, and they had cash for the asking price. The prospective buyers had inherited some money and needed to invest it right away.

On our last Sunday we had the estate sale and cleared out the remaining furniture, antiques, and odds and ends. We had carpets cleaned on Monday and the house professionally cleaned on Tuesday. The deal was closed on Thursday; by Friday the money my mother needed was in her bank, and we were ready to leave.

The Lord prepared in advance for everything we needed: the perfect realtor, a liquidator to hold the estate sale, and a buyer to whom our Designer gave not only the exact amount of money for the house but also a need to invest immediately. "And the Lord, he it is that doth go before thee; he will be with thee, he will not fail thee, neither forsake thee: fear not, neither be dismayed" (Deuteronomy 31:8).

A troubled person once told A.R. Torrey, "I can't believe." Torrey replied, "Whom can't you believe?"[19] Faith does not focus on the circumstances or logic or emotions. It does not look inward. It focuses entirely on the Designer, His promises and His faithfulness. Faith claims the reality that with Him all things are possible, and nothing is too hard.

Dig Deeper:

- Does genuine faith dominate your life? Explain your answer.
- What needs have you trusted your Designer for, and how did He supply them?
- What hinders you from living by faith in your daily life?
- Can you trust your Designer enough to thank Him in advance for meeting your needs?

My Thoughts:

_____

_____

_____

_____

_____

_____

_____

_____

_____

_____

DAY 2
WHAT IS NOT BIBLICAL FAITH

There are various misconceptions about faith and what it means to walk by it. Yesterday we studied in detail about genuine, biblical faith. It does not coincide with human logic. What our Designer tells us often goes directly against our reasoning.

"For whoever will save his life shall lose it: but whoever will lose his life for my sake shall find it" (Matthew 16:25). "Give and it shall be given unto you" (Luke 6:38). "Love your enemies, do good to them which hate you, bless those that curse you, and pray for them which spitefully use you" (Luke 6:27). These commands make no sense and contradict human logic.

Some may say faith is like crossing your fingers and hoping everything will be all right. Others think faith is merely the power of positive thinking. Such views do not describe genuine faith.

Remember, at the beginning of this lesson we said the validity of faith depends on the reliability of its object. Any idea about faith based on our emotions is unreliable. Nothing is more unstable than our emotions, and building our faith on them is like building on shifting sand.

Paul stated in 2 Corinthians 5:7 that believers should walk by faith and not by sight. Does this statement mean we are blind to what is going on around us or that we live in a fantasy world? The answer is no.

It does mean we view the world from a different standpoint. We endeavor to walk and live with a spiritual perspective of life. "While we look not at the things which are seen, but at the things which are not seen: for the things which are seen are temporal; but the things which are not seen are eternal" (2 Corinthians 4:18).

Since we know everything in this world is unstable and will one day decay or be destroyed, it does not determine our purpose or goals. We focus on the spiritual need of those around us instead of on their sinful lifestyle.

We live and interact with this world, the society around us, but keep our Designer's guidelines in mind. "Seek those things which are above...set your affections on things above" (Colossians 3:1-2). "Seek ye first the kingdom of God and his righteousness" (Matthew 6:33).

Having faith does not mean we have all the answers or that we never doubt. It means we turn to our Designer, who does have all the answers. It means we can humbly pray even as the father of a demon-possessed boy prayed in Mark 9:24: "Lord, I believe; help thou my unbelief!"

Genuine, biblical faith does not rest on what our human mind sees as possible, but solely on the power and authority of our Designer. Faith unlocks the door to miracles.

Dig Deeper:
- Describe faith in your own words.
- Have you had any misconceptions about faith? If so, what were they?
- How would you describe a spiritual perspective?
- How do you think keeping a spiritual perspective would affect the way you live?
- Do you struggle with believing God? If yes, why? Write out your answer.

My Thoughts:

_____
_____
_____
_____
_____
_____
_____
_____
_____
_____
_____
_____
_____
_____
_____
_____
_____
_____
_____
_____
_____
_____
_____
_____
_____

_____

_____

_____

_____

_____

_____

_____

_____

_____

_____

_____

_____

_____

_____

_____

_____

_____

_____

_____

_____

_____

_____

_____

_____

_____

_____

_____

_____

_____

DAY 3
FAITH MUST BE TESTED

When I was in nurse's training, I attended all the class lectures, took notes, and spent large amounts of time studying. By the end of the semester, I felt pretty confident about the material the teachers had covered over the preceding months. Now the day of the final test arrived. No problem. I had studied and felt prepared.

But when I sat down with the exam and began to read my confidence slowly melted away. The questions did not require simple facts. They were essay questions requiring application and deduction. It was not as I expected, and it quickly revealed I did not know as much as I thought I did.

We may have a relationship with our Designer and possess a certain amount of Bible knowledge and faith. We find it easy to assure a friend who lost her job that God will provide for her need. But are we just as confident when we lose our job? It is easy to feel confident about our faith until it gets put to the test.

The world desperately needs Christians who can speak with genuine conviction and certainty about God and His Word. For this reason, our Designer orchestrates situations to test and strengthen our faith. D. L. Moody said, "Our great problem is of trafficking in unlived truth. We try to communicate what we've never experienced in our own life."[20]

When our grandson was young and started weightlifting, he could not handle much. But he did not give up. He continued working on it, and every week or so he would add a few more pounds of weight. The more he exercised and exerted his strength, the stronger he became.

Each test our Designer brings into our lives requires us to stretch a little farther, to endure a little more, and to deepen our level of trust in Him. These times of testing not only deepen our faith but change our character. "Knowing this, that the trying of your faith worketh patience. But let patience have her perfect work, that ye may be perfect and entire, wanting nothing" (James 1:3). They work to mature us spiritually.

In the middle of these testing times, our natural tendency is to focus on the situation, how hard it is, and perhaps even doubt whether we can get through it. If we allow our minds to stay fixed on the WAVES and the WIND, we will sink.

In contrast, if we stretch our faith, fixing our mind on the faithfulness of our Designer and His promises, we will experience spiritual power and find we can WALK ON THE WATER. "Looking unto Jesus the author and finisher of our faith" (Hebrews 12:2). "I can do all things through Christ which strengtheneth me" (Philippians 4:13).

The life of Abraham provides a good illustration of how testing can grow faith. When God first spoke to Abram, God commanded him to leave his land and his family and travel to an unknown destination. Abram obeyed, or at least partially.

Abram did leave his homeland and exercised considerable faith by packing up his family and possessions and setting out on a journey with an unknown destination. He did not fully obey because he took his nephew, Lot, after God had told him to leave his family behind.

In the process of time, the Designer changed Abram's name to Abraham. During the ensuing forty to forty-five years, Abraham's faith grew. It was tested time and time again, and now the stage was set for the ultimate test. "And he said, Take now thy son, thine only *son* Isaac, whom thou lovest, and get thee into the land of Moriah; and offer him there for a burnt offering upon one of the mountains which I will tell thee of" (Genesis 22:2).

When Abraham heard this unexpected command from his Designer, he acted immediately. He did not argue, procrastinate, or refuse. Neither did he respond with human reasoning or emotions or seek the advice of others. Only a faith that had been tested over time and made strong could respond as Abraham did.

"And Abraham rose up early in the morning, and saddled his ass, and took two of his young men with him, and Isaac his son, and clave the wood for the burnt offering, and rose up and went unto the place of which God had told him" (Genesis 22:3).

Abraham did not know his Designer would provide the ram. In fact, he had no idea what his Designer was going to do, but he did know he could trust Him. Abraham's faith was not grounded in what he understood or felt. It was grounded in the One he knew so well, his Designer.

If we read the rest of the story, we know Abraham did not need to sacrifice his son because his Designer provided a ram instead. It was a test of Abraham's faith, and he passed.

When our Designer leads us to change directions in our life, step out of our comfort zone, or watch our children move out on their own, it requires faith—genuine *pistis* faith. It requires us to submit to His will in assurance of His loving care.

Times of testing are not easy, but they are necessary to strengthen our faith and make our testimony powerful. They are necessary for us to experience the reality of our Designer in our life.

Dig Deeper:

- What effect do you think Abraham's actions had on Isaac and the servants that accompanied them?
- How has your Designer tested your faith?
- Do you believe God can keep His promises? Do you believe He will keep them for you? If not, why not?

- What sort of experiences have made your faith stronger?

My Thoughts:

_____

_____

_____

_____

_____

_____

_____

_____

_____

_____

_____

_____

_____

_____

_____

_____

_____

_____

_____

_____

_____

_____

_____

_____

DAY 4
FRUIT OF GENUINE FAITH

Genuine faith will result in spiritual growth and change. In John 15, our Designer compares our relationship with Him to a vine and its branches. This parable illustrates that a life living by faith, in close communion with his Designer, will produce spiritual fruit. "I am the vine, ye are the branches. He that abideth in me, and I in him, the same bringeth forth much fruit; for without me ye can do nothing" (John 15:5).

In nature, only a healthy branch can produce fruit. For a branch to be healthy, it needs large doses of sunshine, rain, and proper nutrients from the vine. Similarly, we need to be spiritually healthy if we want to produce fruit. We, too, need lots of time in the Son's presence, the work of the Holy Spirit in our hearts, and good spiritual food.

David recognized the importance of his relationship with his Designer and greatly desired it. "My soul longeth, yea, even fainteth for the courts of the Lord: my heart and my flesh cry out for the living God" (Psalm 84:2).

We also need spiritual nourishment, and the Bible will provide an abundant supply. Nothing this world can offer us will increase our faith. Quite the contrary, input from the world will most often inject doubt and fear, which will decrease our faith.

Fellowship with other believers, listening to good sermons, and reading devotional books or how-to books on Christian living certainly have their place, and they can be a help. But nothing can replace reading the Bible for ourselves and allowing the Holy Spirit to speak to our hearts.

If we want to produce spiritual fruit, then the Word of God is a must. "It is written, Man shall not live by bread alone, but by every word that proceedeth out of the mouth of God" (Matthew 4:4).

When we nourish our spirits in communion with our Designer and His Word, we will be healthy branches through which the Holy Spirit can produce His fruit: a Christ-like character. "But the fruit of the Spirit is love, joy, peace, longsuffering, gentleness, goodness, faith, meekness, temperance: against such there is no law" (Galatians 5:22, 23).

Genuine faith produces the fruit of prayer. According to E. M. Bounds, faith ceases to live when it ceases to pray. Unwavering trust in our Designer will draw our hearts to pour out all our needs and intercede for the needs of others in prayer.

When we pray, we have a personal, private time with our Designer, with the Lord of lords and King of kings. Just think about it. At that moment you have Him all to yourself. His attention is on you, and He is listening to what you are saying. You have the opportunity to share with your Designer, one-on-one, your deepest fears, desires, and emotions. What a priceless privilege!

Prayer also allows us to worship and praise our Designer and express our gratitude for who He is and the multitude of blessings we have. "Enter His gates with thanksgiving, and into his courts with praise: be thankful unto him, and bless his name" (Psalm 100:4).

Since prayer is a conversation, it goes two ways. Therefore, it is essential for us not just to talk to our Designer, but to be still, listen, and allow Him to speak to us. This requires time...time investing in a relationship.

Faith produces the fruit of good works. The word *good* could describe all sorts of works: social, humanitarian, financial, or medical. What kind of good works does genuine faith produce?

Paul talked to the church at Colossae about this very subject. In Colossians 1:4 he talks about their faith in Christ and their love for all other believers. Then in verse 9 he encourages them to be filled with godly wisdom and spiritual understanding. In verse 10 Paul says these things will make them fruitful in every good work.

Therefore, we can conclude that the fruit of good works are those produced by love, wisdom, and spiritual understanding. They are the works directed by the Holy Spirit. It is especially important that the good works we do are not just our good idea but are the will of our Designer.

I learned this lesson the hard way. My brain is always coming up with ideas, and they all seem good to me. When I was a young pastor's wife, if I thought it would be good to make a cake or some other dish for a neighbor or shut-in, I just did it. After all, that is a good work. Sadly, not everyone agreed with me, and the reaction I received was not always what I expected or desired.

Now I have learned to pray first. I ask the Lord to show me if my good idea is from Him or simply my thought. Sometimes the idea is just mine, and I have learned when this is the case to drop it. Taking time to ask our Designer about our ideas will minimize disappointments, wasted time, and energy.

James says faith without works is dead. "Yea, a man may say, thou hast faith, and I have works: shew me thy faith without thy works, and I will show you my faith by my works" (James 2:18). The good works of genuine faith are those works done in obedience to our Designer's leading.

Dig Deeper:
- What kind of fruit is your faith producing in your life?
- Why do you read the Bible? How does reading it affect your daily life?

- How would you describe your prayer life? Have you learned to be still and listen?
- What good works has your Designer led you to do in the last month?

My Thoughts:

_____

_____

_____

_____

_____

_____

_____

_____

_____

_____

_____

_____

_____

_____

_____

_____

_____

_____

_____

_____

_____

_____

_____

_____

DAY 5
WAYS TO INCREASE OUR FAITH

We have covered a lot about faith in this chapter, and if you are like me, you realize your faith needs to increase. We know our Designer brings circumstances into our lives to grow our faith, but what can we do in a practical way to increase or strengthen our faith?

Romans 10:17 gives us direction. "So then faith cometh by hearing, and hearing by the word of God." One of the primary keys to increasing our faith is the Bible. We not only need to read it but to study and memorize it.

Memorizing does not come easy for some of us and may grow even harder as we age. The verses I can remember the best are the ones I memorized as a child. It may not come easy for us, and it will take time and effort; but it is valuable. We do not always have time to look up a verse in our Bible or on our cell phone. It needs to be in our minds and available when we need it as our sword against Satan's attacks.

It is the remembered Word that calms us when a nightmare awakens us. It is the comfort that soothes us when we are too sick or too weak to read. It fortifies us when we are walking into a threatening situation. Memorizing God's Word equips us for the unexpected and keeps us from sin. "Thy word have I hid in my heart that I might not sin against thee" (Psalm 119:11).

Meditation on Scripture will increase our faith. Meditation is quite popular in today's world. I typed it into google and found meditation pillows, rugs, oils, classes, videos, exercises, and music. Most of the time it seemed connected to a deeper life or some Eastern religion.

What is meditation, and how do we do it? To meditate simply means to contemplate or think over something. We rerun the past and think about the future. We think about all the "what if" and "if only" scenarios of our lives. Worry and fretting are nothing more than meditating on the negative. We do it every day.

When we read a verse of Scripture we can stop and think about what it is saying. Is it a command, a warning, or a promise? Is it an event or example from history? Does it reveal something about our Designer or His character? What does it have to do with me?

In the Psalms David often mentions meditating on his Designer: "When I remember thee upon my bed, and meditate on thee in the *night* watches" (Psalm 63:6). "I remember the days of old; I meditate on all thy works; I muse on the work of thy hands" (Psalm 143:5).

After the death of Moses, our Designer put Joshua in the position of leadership. He gave Joshua clear instructions that emphasized the importance of knowing and meditating on God's Word. "This Book of the Law shall not depart out of your mouth; but thou shalt meditate therein day and night, that thou mayest observe to do according to all that is written therein: for then thou shalt make thy way prosperous, and thou shalt have good success" (Joshua 1:8).

Thinking about Scripture will direct our thoughts in a godly direction and help us make wise decisions. "The entrance of thy words giveth light; it giveth understanding unto the simple" (Psalm 119:130). It will bring about spiritual change as well as growth in our faith.

Being an active member of a Bible preaching/teaching church is another way to grow our faith. When specific verses or Bible passages are read and expounded upon and perhaps related to other scriptural references, they become more meaningful. Understanding Scripture better will deepen our trust of our Designer.

Reading biographies of people secure in faith can help us grow. One of my favorite biographies is that of George Mueller. He was known primarily for his faith. He took all his material needs to his Designer in prayer and then depended on Him to supply them. The care of his orphanages gave evidence to this faith. The following incident recorded in his autobiographical entry for February 12, 1842, reveals the kind of relationship George had with his Designer and the depth of his faith.

"One morning the plates and cups and bowls on the table were empty. There was no food in the cabinet and no money to buy food. The children were standing waiting for their morning meal when Mueller said, 'Children, you know we must be in time for school.' Lifting his hand, he said, 'Dear Father, we thank Thee for what Thou art going to give us to eat.'

"There was a knock on the door. The baker stood there, and said, 'Mr. Mueller, I couldn't sleep last night. Somehow, I felt you didn't have bread for breakfast and the Lord wanted me to send you some. So I got up at 2 a.m. and baked some fresh bread and have brought it.' Mueller thanked the man.

"No sooner had this transpired when there was a second knock at the door. It was the milkman. He announced that his milk cart had broken down right in front of the orphanage, and he would like to give the children his cans of fresh milk so he could empty his wagon and repair it."[21]

No wonder, years later, when Mueller was to travel the world as an evangelist, he would be heralded as "the man who gets things from God"!

How could he be so convinced his Designer would supply all his needs? He saturated his mind and soul with God's Word and spent quality time in prayer every day. The things that gave George Mueller his strong faith can also increase our faith.

Dig Deeper:

- What need are you trusting your Designer to supply?
- If the only Bible you had for the rest of your life were the verses you knew by memory, how much would you have?
- What do you think about when you are alone or when trying to fall asleep? What do you meditate on?
- What biographies have you read that have influenced your faith?
- What steps can you take to increase your faith?

My Thoughts:

_____

_____

_____

_____

_____

_____

_____

_____

_____

_____

_____

_____

_____

_____

_____

_____

_____

Chapter Seven
WHAT IS OUR RESPONSIBILITY?

We have learned our Designer, Jesus Christ, not only has a purpose for each of us, but He also divinely orchestrates the pieces needed in our individual puzzles and their timing. We understand the importance and wisdom of following the leadership of Christ in all the decisions we face, since He alone knows the future and the design of our life puzzle.

In short, we have talked about all the things our Designer does in our life. Now we ask, what is our responsibility? How much is left to us?

The various religions in the world have diverse ideas about the answers to these two questions. Some say God demands sacrifice, while others claim He desires isolation and poverty. Yet others maintain our Designer is a hard taskmaster and requires us to live according to strict rules and hard punishment with little or no freedom of choice.

Whatever the religion or philosophy might be they can offer no assurance of forgiveness or eternal life. They provide no way for their followers to develop an intimate relationship with the one who created them. The followers are held by fear, never having a secure future.

Our Designer holds His followers with love…unconditional love. He loved us first and proved it by His sacrifice on the cross. "We love him, because he first loved us" (1 John 4:19).

He has given us life and promises to carry our burdens, guide our decisions, and meet every need as we trust and follow Him. Our Designer said, "I am come that they might have life, and that they might have it more abundantly" (John 10:10). He gives us so much. What can we give Him?

DAY 1
WALK IN HUMILITY

In our society, humility is not generally at the top of the list for desired character traits. In fact, it is viewed as a weakness and not a quality needed for success. Successful people are known for their self-confidence, assertiveness, and passionate drive to reach their goals. For God's children, though, there can be no biblical change, no spiritual growth, without humility.

Why is humility so imperative? The answer is simple. The opposite of humility is pride, and pride stems from self-dependence and resistance to the lordship of our Designer. A life puzzle dominated by pride will never accomplish what it was designed to be.

Why does our Designer want us to be humble before Him? He loves us intensely and wants not only to bless us but to have a close relationship with us. Without humility this is impossible.

He desires us to accomplish what we were designed to do. Spiritual success can only happen when we deliberately and willingly recognize who we are and who He is. As Andrew Murray said, "Humility is simply acknowledging the truth of our position and yielding to God His position."[22]

Humility before our Designer is accepting our unworthiness and dependence. It is acknowledging that all we have He has given us. "Every good gift and every perfect gift is from above, and cometh down from the Father of lights" (James 1:17).

We can do nothing except what He enables us to do. We are dependent by design, and humility willingly accepts this fact. "I am the vine, and ye are the branches. …for without me, ye can do nothing" (John 15:5).

But humility does not come naturally to us. Our flesh likes to feel independent and self-sufficient. When I was young, I knew I was dependent on my Designer in some areas of life, but in other areas I felt self-sufficient. My Designer saw my foolishness and knew how to show me how wrong I was. He has various ways to expose our dependence.

He can give us a problem we cannot handle or solve with our understanding. It may be dealing with a rebellious teenager or caring for an aging parent. It might be a complicated work situation or a difficult relationship. Whatever it may be, it will make our insufficiency clear.

Our Designer can give us a command that will expose our self-centeredness. It may involve forgiving someone we resent. He may call us to leave our comfort zone and all that is familiar to step out into the unknown. The command may be to do something we never wanted to do. Such commands can quickly reveal a prideful and rebellious heart.

Hidden sin may result in an outcome we can't control and did not expect. Satan likes to convince us we can sin "in secret" with no negative results. But no sins are secret with our Designer, and although repentance does bring mercy, He designs the consequences to humble our arrogance. When people discover what we never wanted them to know, it can be very humbling.

Whatever it takes, our Designer knows how to reveal a self-ruling mindset. When these circumstances come, we msut make a choice. We can continue to resist and rebel in our self-centeredness, or we can repent and humble ourselves before our loving, righteous Designer.

The reason for the humbling pieces in our life puzzle is not to push us further down, but to bring us up to the place of blessing. "Humble yourself in the sight of the Lord, and he shall lift you up" (James 4:10).

We have already learned that our Designer is our role-model for a godly life, and this includes having a humble spirit. To obey His Father, Jesus was willing to leave the realms of glory where He was honored and worshipped and to take on the form of a mortal man.

Our Designer knew the rejection, mocking, and denial He would be called to endure. He knew He would suffer excruciating pain and mental anguish to become the sacrifice for our sins, but He willingly obeyed. "And being found in fashion as a man, he humbled himself, and became obedient unto death, even the death of the cross" (Philippians 2:8).

Jesus, the Creator of all things, humbled Himself to obey whatever His Father wanted Him to do regardless of the cost. This same attitude is what our Designer desires from us. "Let this mind be in you which was also in Christ Jesus" (Philippians 2:5).

"He hath shewed thee, O man, what us good; and what doth the Lord require of thee, but to do justly, and to love mercy, and to walk humbly with thy God?" (Micah 6:8).

Dig Deeper:

- Write out what Micah 6:8 means to you.
- How do you feel about the responsibility of humility? Write out your thoughts.
- Read the following verses and make a list of the blessings of a humble spirit. Psalm 25:9; Proverbs 3:24, 11:2, 22:4; James 4:10; 1 Peter 5:6
- Do you struggle with having a humble spirit toward your Designer? If so, what do you think is your greatest hindrance?
- Read the following verses and explain how humility affects our relationships with others. Philippines 11:2; Ephesians 4:2; 1 Peter 3:8

My Thoughts:

_____

_____

_____

_____

_____

_____

_____

_____

_____

DAY 2
UNCONDITIONAL SURRENDER

When we realize that all we are and all we have are wrapped in the undeserved, redeeming love of our Designer, we will not only be humbled, but we will surrender to His will.

The word *surrender* does not often carry a good connotation. It can imply quitting or giving up on a goal or project. It may mean stopping all efforts to overcome a disease or disability. In war it means losing to the one who is stronger and more powerful and indicates defeat with no hope for victory. Surrender in our society indicates loss and can result in feelings of guilt or shame.

Spiritual surrender works quite differently. It is a willing, decisive, deliberate decision to accept the authority, power, and ownership of our Designer. It is not a sign of defeat but is, in fact, just the opposite. It is the key to fulfilling our destiny. "Commit thy way unto the Lord; trust also in him; and he shall bring it to pass" (Psalm 27:5).

Our old nature is obsessed with having control and, therefore, resists surrendering to our Designer. We may hear our enemy whisper that surrendering will result in losing what we want, what we hold dear, or what makes us happy. We should not forget that our enemy is the father of lies and is after our destruction.

As a young girl, I surrendered my life to my Designer: *Lord, whatever You want, I will do, and wherever You want me to go, I will go.* My desire was sincere, but I did not yet understand what this decision would mean or what it would involve. It did not take long for me to realize the decision to surrender was mine, but I could not accomplish what this would entail in my power.

I felt like Paul when he shared his dilemma. He did what he did not want to do and what he wanted to do was not what happened (Romans 7:15-16). My struggle continued for some years. I told my Designer that I felt as if He dangled the victorious life like a carrot in front of me, knowing I would never attain it. I was ignorant, self-willed, and so wrong.

To come to the place of surrender, I first had to recognize the power my old nature had in my life. Then I needed to acknowledge and claim the truth that my Designer had set me free from its power. Romans, chapter 6, explains this to us. Since my time is limited in this study to pursue this teaching in-depth, I would suggest you study this chapter at another time for yourself, asking the Holy Spirit to guide you and give you clarity.

When we accept Jesus Christ as our Savior, we are in Him, and He is in us. "To them God would make known what *is* the riches of the glory of this mystery among the Gentiles; which is Christ in you, the hope of glory" (Colossians 1:27).

By this divine, supernatural transaction, we are set free from the bondage of sin. "Knowing this, that our old man is crucified with *him*, that the body of sin might be destroyed, that henceforth we should not serve sin" (Romans 6:6).

In verse 6, the Greek word translated "done away with" does not mean "any longer existing" but rather to "render inoperative." We are now free to yield to our Designer. We no longer have to yield to our old nature's sinful desires and habits—we have a choice.

This truth was not easy for me to grasp until I read a word picture describing its meaning. I do not remember where I read it, but I want to share it and hope it will also help you.

Imagine we are the crew of a sailing ship on the high seas. Our captain is cruel, wicked, and demanding. We have been under his authority and domination for years and are accustomed to hearing his harsh commands and feeling the sting of his merciless whip.

Then something remarkable happens. The captain is found guilty of crimes by a court in a far-away country and relieved of his command. Until we reach port, he is stripped of his position and authority and chained in the bottom of the ship.

Meanwhile, a new captain comes on board. He is loving, patient, and just. He takes a personal interest in each of us and promises to take care of us. We have never known such love. But we can still hear the old captain yelling out his demands and threats. Now we must choose. We can continue to fear and heed the ranting of our old evil captain, who no longer has any authority over us, or we can choose to tell him no and yield our allegations and obedience to our new captain. The choice is ours.

Romans 6:11 says we are to reckon ourselves dead unto sin and alive to God. What does it mean to reckon something true? The word *reckon* is both a term of faith and a term of reality. It means "to consider, to believe, and to claim something personally true." We can choose to believe God's Word, which says we are free from the bondage of sin, or we can continue believing the lie that we have no choice.

This truth allows us the privilege of surrendering unconditionally to our Designer. "Neither yield ye your members as instruments of unrighteousness unto sin, but yield yourselves unto God, as those that are alive from the dead, and your members as instruments of righteousness unto God" (Romans 6:13).

Yielding ourselves to our Designer is not a one-time decision, but something we will need to do every day. What does our Designer want from us? He wants us to accept the complete truth of His atonement for our sins and surrender all our rights.

Dig Deeper:

- "I beseech you therefore, brethren, by the mercies of God, that ye present your bodies a living sacrifice, holy, acceptable unto God, which is your reasonable service" (Romans 12:1). What does this verse mean to you?
- What do you think Romans 6:6 means? How can the reality of this verse change your life?
- Have you come to the place of unconditional surrender? If not, what is holding you back?
- What effect do you think our surrender has on our service for our Designer, on our relationship with Him?

My Thoughts:

_____

_____

_____

_____

_____

_____

_____

_____

_____

_____

_____

_____

_____

_____

_____

_____

_____

_____
_____
_____
_____
_____
_____
_____
_____
_____
_____
_____
_____
_____
_____
_____
_____
_____
_____
_____
_____
_____
_____
_____
_____
_____
_____
_____
_____
_____
_____
_____

DAY 3
ALL-INCLUSIVE LOVE

"Do you love me?" Jesus asked Peter this direct question. What if Jesus were standing in front of you and me asking the same question? What would we say?

We might quickly respond, "Of course, we love You, Lord," or we might hesitate, searching our own hearts for the truth. We know we should love our Designer and are commanded to do so. In fact, both in the Old Testament (Deuteronomy 6:5) and in the New Testament (Mark 12:30), we are told to love God with all our heart, soul, mind, and strength. We might think this is impossible, but our Designer never gives us a command we cannot fulfill in His power.

The love spoken of in Mark 12:30 is *Agape* love. This kind of love is much more than sentimental emotions. It is a committed, self-sacrificing, unconditional love. It is the kind of love God the Father had for us when He sent His beloved Son, Jesus Christ, to die for our sins. It is the kind of love described in 1 Corinthians 13. Unconditional love is never dependent on or affected by what we do or do not do.

It stands to reason that our old sinful nature could never love our Designer with this kind of love, so how can we obey this commandment? We can love our Designer because He gives us His love. "Because the love of God is shed abroad in our hearts by the Holy Ghost which is given unto us" (Romans 5:5). *Agape* love can only come from our Designer Himself.

To follow the commandment we mentioned initially, however, our love must intensify, which is up to us. The commandment is easier to understand if we take the verse apart. We are to love our Designer with all our hearts. This phrase refers to our sincerity. We are to love our Designer with singleness of heart, intentionally and determinedly.

Many verses in both the Old Testament and New Testament stress the importance of loving God with our whole heart. "And thou shalt love the Lord thy God with all thine heart, and with all thy soul, and with all thy might" (Deuteronomy 6:5).

We are to love our Designer with all our soul or with our emotions. We are to love Him with passion and dedication, which annuls a lukewarm or indifferent attitude. When our focus centers not on us or what we are doing, but on our Designer and developing an intimate relationship with Him, our passion for serving will intensify. The closer we are to our Designer, the deeper we will experience His love in us and, in turn, love Him more.

Paul wanted the church at Ephesus to experience a more profound love for Christ. He desired for them "to know the love of Christ, which passeth knowledge" (Ephesians 3:19). This depth of love only comes from experiencing it, not in intellectual knowledge.

To love our Designer with all our souls, we must allow Him to fill our very being, creating a driving passion for dedicating ourselves freely for His service.

We are to love Him with all our mind or intellect. We can grow in our love for our Designer as we read and study His Word. The Holy Spirit will work to renew our minds and give us a spiritual insight into what we are reading. Saturating our minds with the truth of God's Word influences how we think.

We can do this not only by reading the Bible, but also by reading literature and listening to music that helps us focus on our Designer, His attributes, and His promises. They can also help us avoid things that would divert our love from our Designer.

To love with all our strength involves activity and energy. It means spending our energy, time, and talents in doing those things that bring Him glory. But it means even more than that. It means doing what we do as if we were doing it for Him personally. Let me illustrate what I mean.

When our people bought our church building, it was just a large building without Sunday school rooms, a kitchen, or a fellowship hall. Much remodeling work lay ahead of us. If you have ever remodeled an old building, you can imagine the resulting mess of chipped plaster, spilled concrete, and powder-fine dust.

Often my husband and I were the ones left to do the clean-up work. I remember being on my hands and knees scraping plaster off the floor and complaining, *Where is everyone else? It is not just our church. They want it cleaned up on Sunday, but where are they now?*

Then it was as if I heard the Lord say, "Sandy, if I lived here, would You mind cleaning My floors?" Immediately my heart responded, *No, Lord. I would be thrilled to clean Your floors.* I got His point.

From that moment on, any time I clean at the church, I imagine doing it directly for Him as if He physically lived there. This picture changes my whole attitude about it and gives me joy.

Personal experience has shown that gratitude plays a large role in the intensity of my love for my Designer. The more I comprehend the depth of my sinfulness (through the work of the Holy Spirit), the more thankful I am for my salvation. My thankfulness, in turn, deepens my love.

Luke 7:4 gives us an example of this truth. It tells of a sinful woman who washed Jesus' feet with her tears and wiped them with her hair. "Therefore, I say to you, her sins, which are many, are forgiven, for she loved much. But to whom little is forgiven, the same loves little."

As our relationship with our Designer deepens, our love for Him will deepen, which will become evident through our obedience. Jesus said, "If ye love me, keep my commandments" (John 14:15). No one loves us more than our Designer, and no one deserves our love more than He does.

Dig Deeper:

- Do you serve your Designer with singlemindedness? If not, what is causing you to be double-minded?
- On a scale from one to ten, with ten being the highest, how passionate are you about your Designer?
- Are you allowing the Holy Spirit to renew your mind through reading God's Word? If yes, give an example. If not, why not?
- What do your activities, music, and pastime activities reveal about your priorities?
- Has your love for your Designer grown this last year? How does your life reflect this?

My Thoughts:

_____

_____

_____

_____

_____

_____

_____

_____

DAY 4
UNQUESTIONING OBEDIENCE

Obedience is so simple young children can accomplish it. It is not complicated, nor does it require great ability, wealth, or extensive knowledge. It involves merely following the instructions given by the one in authority. If it is simple, then why do we often find it hard to obey our Designer?

One reason could be that obeying our Designer often requires us to change our plans and surrender our will. Since our old nature resists surrender, we may find ways to counterfeit obedience. Counterfeiting means to do the right things but for the wrong reasons.

We can regularly go to church, sing in the choir, give money in the offering, help organize events, and do various other activities but with wrong motives. Our motivation may be to meet others' expectations, fit in with our peers, or satisfy our emotional need for recognition and praise. This kind of outward behavior may fool those around us, but it will not deceive or impress our Designer. He knows our real intent. "I, the Lord, search the heart, I try the reins" (Jeremiah 17:10). He knows our every thought.

Obedience will not react like Jonah. God told Jonah to go to Nineveh and warn them of impending judgment if they did not repent of their wickedness. Jonah refused to obey the Lord's command and caught a ship going in the opposite direction from the city. Jonah knew God was merciful, and he did not want forgiveness for the people of Nineveh. He wanted God's judgment to fall on them.

We may rebel at the Lord's leading in our lives for a similar reason. We don't want to forgive that person who caused us pain and anguish of heart. We don't want to love our critical neighbors who spread lies about us and our family. We rebel because what our Designer wants goes against what we want.

Disobedience is not always saying a blatant no. One of our grandchildren was talking to my husband on the day of my father's funeral. He asked, if he intended to get saved but had not yet done it when he died, would that count? My husband told him no, his good intentions would not substitute for accepting Christ as his Savior. Procrastination is not obedience.

We might be like Gideon. When the Lord spoke to him about saving Israel, Gideon responded with excuses for why this could not be possible. "O my Lord, wherewith shall I save Israel? Behold my family is poor in Manasseh, and I am the least in my father's house" (Judges 6:15).

When we hear the Lord's command and then look at ourselves and all our inabilities, weaknesses, and hindrances, our response can quickly be a list of excuses explaining why we cannot obey.

On the other hand, we might be so full of zeal that we run ahead of the Lord. Moses did just that. He saw his brethren suffering under the hand of an Egyptian, and in his good intentions he killed the Egyptian and hid the body.

What he thought would help backfired, however, and resulted in Moses landing on the desert's backside for forty years. His desire to help his people was not wrong, but Moses acted without waiting for God's timing and instructions.

A missionary translator was endeavoring to find a word for obedience in a native language. This was a virtue seldom practiced among the people into whose language he wanted to translate the New Testament. As he returned home from the village one day, he whistled for his dog, and it came running at full speed. An old native, seeing this, said admiringly in the native tongue, "Your dog is all ear." Immediately the missionary knew he had his word for obedience.

Psalm 5:3 says, "My voice shalt thou hear in the morning, O Lord; in the morning will I direct my prayer unto thee, and will look up." This verse translated into English from the German Schlachter 2000 Bible says, "Early will I look up and stand ready for your orders."

Are we "all ear" when our Designer speaks to us? Are we consciously, purposefully, ready to do what our Designer wants when our day begins?

Dig Deeper:

- Have there been times you were not obedient to your Designer? What did He want you to do? Why do you think you disobeyed?
- What commands in God's Word do you find hard to obey?
- Read John 14:21-24. According to these verses, what do you think obedience says to our Designer?
- According to 1 Samuel 15:22-23, how does your Designer view disobedience?
- Read 1John 3:22. How does obedience affect our prayers?

My Thoughts:

_____

_____

_____

_____

_____

_____

_____

_____

_____
_____
_____
_____
_____
_____
_____
_____
_____
_____
_____
_____
_____
_____
_____
_____
_____
_____
_____
_____
_____
_____
_____
_____
_____
_____
_____
_____

DAY 5
SERVANT'S HEART

Our Designer is our role model, and His life exemplifies what it means to be a servant. "For even the Son of man came not to be ministered unto, but to minister, and to give his life a ransom for many" (Mark 10:45).

Our Designer knows how we struggle with taking the position of a servant, so He demonstrated it for us consistently in His life. His sacrifice on the cross was a powerful example of love and service. But He did another act that exemplifies the entire concept of being a servant.

Let your mind go back in time and try to picture this scene. Our Designer has just finished eating with His disciples. They are probably chit-chatting with one another when the Designer stands up. As the attention of the disciples shifts to Him, the Designer takes off His outer garment, grabs a towel, and ties it around Himself. Now He gets a basin of water and kneels before the feet of the nearest disciple. Taken aback, surprised, and perhaps bewildered, the disciples wonder what their Master is doing.

Here we see the one who created all things, walked on water, stilled the storm, healed the sick, cast out demons, and fed thousands—the one who continually did the impossible, the miraculous, doing the work of an ordinary servant. The incarnate Christ willingly, lovingly washes the dirty feet of His unworthy disciples—all the while knowing Judas would betray Him, Peter would deny Him, and the others would desert Him.

This scene is flooded with emotion and powerful meaning. The Designer's act of service was based solely on love and not on His disciples' worthiness. When Jesus finished, He said, "For I have given you an example, that ye should do as I have done to you" (John 13:15).

I believe the example our Designer wanted them to follow included more than literally washing one another's feet. It was the example of being willing to do whatever they could for others in unconditional love.

This example applies to us today. Willingly yielding and obeying our Designer by doing the humble servant's work fulfills both of our Designer's commandments. The first was to love Him above all else, and the other was to love our neighbor as ourselves.

What will a servant attitude look like in our life? First, we will not be concerned with position, recognition, or praise. Our joy will not come from the work we do but from knowing we are obedient to our Designer. Jesus said, "If ye know these things, happy are ye if ye do them" (John 13:17).

A servant's heart will be compassionate to others. It is so easy to judge others by what we know or have experienced, by our standards. But we have all experienced life in different ways. If we want to have a compassionate, servant's heart we will try to put ourselves in the other person's situation. My brother-in-law often said, "I haven't walked in his moccasins, so I don't know what his situation is like."

Compassion does not judge, criticize, or rebuke. It does not allow prejudice or preference to enter in. It seeks to see the person as our Designer views them through the eyes of unconditional love.

Jesus showed compassion to the multitudes who followed Him and had not eaten all day. He showed compassion to the outcast and the ones considered worthless by society. Two blind men cried out for Jesus to heal them, and despite the multitudes who told them to be quiet and go away, Jesus cared about them. "So Jesus had compassion on them, and touched their eyes: and immediately their eyes received sight, and they followed him" (Matthew 20:34).

If we want to be godly servants, then we will put others' needs ahead of our own. We won't insist on our rights or our way but will use all our talents and goods under the Holy Spirit's leadership to edify and encourage other believers. We will be a conduit for the love of our Designer to flow through us to those around us.

From the beginning, our Designer has been working to conform us to His image. "For whom he did foreknow, he also did predestinate to be conformed to the image of his Son that he might be the firstborn among many brethren" (Romans 8:29).

Being in His image is to be like Paul when he said, "I am crucified with Christ: nevertheless I live; but the life which I now live in the flesh I live by the faith of the Son of God, who loved me, and gave himself for me" (Galatians 2:20).

What does our Designer desire from us? He desires a life humbly yielded in love to be His obedient servant. "Being servants of all is the highest fulfillment of our destiny, as a man created in the image of God."[23]

Dig Deeper:
- Imagine your Designer washing your feet. How would this affect you?
- What does being a servant of God mean to you? Find Scripture to support your answers.
- Have you experienced a godly servant in your life? How did that person serve you?
- What do you think hinders believers from becoming servants of one another? What could we do to overcome these hindrances?

My Thoughts:

_____

_____

_____

_____

_____

_____

_____

_____

_____

_____

_____

_____

_____

_____

_____

_____

_____

_____

_____

_____

_____

_____

_____

_____

_____

_____

_____

_____

Conclusion

Now that you've completed this study, I hope you have found the answers to the questions proposed at the beginning and realize how valuable and unique you are. May you be assured that your Designer has carefully crafted in love each piece of your life puzzle to complete the beautiful life He designed and to bring Him glory. My prayer for you is like Paul's desire for the believers at Ephesus.

"That he would grant you, according to the riches of his glory, to be strengthened with might by his Spirit in the inner man; that Christ may dwell in your hearts by faith; that ye, being rooted and grounded in love, may be able to comprehend with all saints what is the breadth, and length, and depth, and height; and to know the love of Christ, which passeth knowledge, that ye might be filled with all the fulness of God" (Ephesians 3:16-19).

If I can be of help to you, please contact me at sandrap.hastings@gmx.de.

About The Author

S andra P. Hastings is an author, international speaker, and Bible teacher who has ministered as a missionary wife in Germany for almost five decades. She has a nursing degree, graduated from Bible College, attended counseling courses, and earned her master's degree in Theology. Sandra has self-published two books: Victory in the Storm, translated into five languages, and Seeing God's Hand, a 52-week Bible study. Sandra's devotions have been featured in Upper Room, on Christian Broadcasting Network, and in the December 2020 issue of Refresh, an online magazine. She has international experience as she has been the speaker/Bible teacher in eleven countries, sends teaching lessons to a national training station in India and writes and teaches Bible lessons and discipleship material in German and English.

References

1   Whitwam, Ryan. "Simulating 1 second of human brain activity takes 82,944 processors." Extremetech.com, August 5, 2013 (retrieved 5/7/2014).

2   Lundgren, A. "Drawing the Line between Art and Design." Alvalyn Studio, September 2016, <alvalyn.com>process-and-outcome>

3   Nick Vujicic—www.imdb.com, biography.

4   Frank Peretti, www.encyclopedia.com, Peretti, Frank E. 1951.

5   Ross, H. "Anthropic Principle: A Precise Plan for Humanity." January 1, 2002 <reasons.org/explore/publications/facts-for-faith>

6   "What Is Mercy? Bible Verses and Meaning," originally published March 25, 2019; https://www.Christianity.com/wiki/Chrisi-tian-terms/what-is-mercy-why-is-it-important.html

7   utmost.org/the-go-of-relationship, 25 Sep 2020

8   Oswald Chambers, *My Utmost for His Highest* (Grand Rapids, MI: Discovery House Pub, 1995).

9   inspiringquotes.us/author/9496-oswald chambers/about bless-ings

10   brainyquote.com/quotes/jm_elliot_189251

11   "The Comparison Trap," Rebecca Webber, *Psychology Today*, November 7, 2017.

12   Ibid.

13   "7 Scientifically Proven Benefits of Gratitude," posted April 3, 2015; www.psychologytoday.com/us/blog/what-mentally -strong-people-don't-do/2015042

14   *Search for Significance*, Joseph M. Stowell, p. 85, Perilous Pursuits.

15   "Forgiveness Is Strength and Forgiveness Is a Disease," www.linkedin.com>pluse>forgiveness-strength-unforgiveness-disease-muhammad-harris-jahangir

16   "Your Health Depends on It," www.hopkinsmedicine.org>wellness-and-prevention>forgiveness

17   utmost.org.the-price-of-the-vision/

18   Lettie B. Cowman, Steams in the Desert, (Los Ageles, CA: The Oriental Missionary Society, 1925), 114

19   Psalm 40:9-Vers-by-Verse Bible Commentary -Studylight, 1 August the-go-of-relationship, 25 Sep 2020

20   https://www.preceptaustin.org/the/key/inductive-study-pt3

21   en.wikipedia>George_Muller

22   *Humility*, Andrew Murray, Heaven Reigns, www.heavenreigns.com>read>read_humility

23   Ibid.

A free ebook edition is available with the purchase of this book.

To claim your free ebook edition:

1. Visit MorganJamesBOGO.com
2. Sign your name CLEARLY in the space
3. Complete the form and submit a photo of the entire copyright page
4. You or your friend can download the ebook to your preferred device

A **FREE** ebook edition is available for you or a friend with the purchase of this print book.

CLEARLY SIGN YOUR NAME ABOVE

Instructions to claim your free ebook edition:
1. Visit MorganJamesBOGO.com
2. Sign your name CLEARLY in the space above
3. Complete the form and submit a photo of this entire page
4. You or your friend can download the ebook to your preferred device

Print & Digital Together Forever.

Snap a photo

Free ebook

Read anywhere